Financing Corporate Capital Formation

A National Bureau
of Economic Research
Project Report

Financing Corporate Capital Formation

Edited by **Benjamin M. Friedman**

The University of Chicago Press

Chicago and London

Benjamin M. Friedman is professor of economics at Harvard
University and program director for financial markets and monetary
economics at the National Bureau of Economic Research. He is the
author of *Economic Stabilization Policy* and *Monetary Policy in the
United States* and editor of *New Challenges to the Role of Profits, The
Changing Roles of Debt and Equity in Financing U.S. Capital
Formation,* and *Corporate Capital Structures in the United States.*

The University of Chicago Press, Chicago 60637
The University of Chicago Press, Ltd., London
© 1986 by The National Bureau of Economic Research
Printed in the United States of America

95 94 93 92 91 90 89 88 87 86   54321

Library of Congress Cataloging-in-Publication Data
Main entry under title:

Financing corporate capital formation.

(A National Bureau of Economic Research project
report)
Papers presented at a conference held at
Williamsburg, Va., Sept. 20–21, 1984, sponsored by
the National Bureau of Economic Research.
Bibliography: p.
Includes indexes.
1. Corporations—United States—Finance—Congresses.
2. Saving and investment—United States—Congresses.
I. Friedman, Benjamin M.   II. National Bureau of
Economic Research.   III. Series.
HG4061.F53 1986   338.7′4′0973   85-16502
ISBN 0-226-26413-0

Relation of the Directors to the
Work and Publications of the
National Bureau of Economic Research

1. The object of the National Bureau of Economic Research is to ascertain and to present to the public important economic facts and their interpretation in a scientific and impartial manner. The Board of Directors is charged with the responsibility of ensuring that the work of the National Bureau is carried on in strict conformity with this object.

2. The President of the National Bureau shall submit to the Board of Directors, or to its Executive Committee, for their formal adoption all specific proposals for research to be instituted.

3. No research report shall be published by the National Bureau until the President has sent each member of the Board a notice that a manuscript is recommended for publication and that in the President's opinion it is suitable for publication in accordance with the principles of the National Bureau. Such notification will include an abstract or summary of the manuscript's content and a response form for use by those Directors who desire a copy of the manuscript for review. Each manuscript shall contain a summary drawing attention to the nature and treatment of the problem studied, the character of the data and their utilization in the report, and the main conclusions reached.

4. For each manuscript so submitted, a special committee of the Directors (including Directors Emeriti) shall be appointed by majority agreement of the President and Vice Presidents (or by the Executive Committee in case of inability to decide on the part of the President and Vice Presidents), consisting of three Directors selected as nearly as may be one from each general division of the Board. The names of the special manuscript committee shall be stated to each Director when notice of the proposed publication is submitted to him. It shall be the duty of each member of the special manuscript committee to read the manuscript. If each member of the manuscript committee signifies his approval within thirty days of the transmittal of the manuscript, the report may be published. If at the end of that period any member of the manuscript committee withholds his approval, the President shall then notify each member of the Board, requesting approval or disapproval of publication, and thirty days additional shall be granted for this purpose. The manuscript shall then not be published unless at least a majority of the entire Board who shall have voted on the proposal within the time fixed for the receipt of votes shall have approved.

5. No manuscript may be published, though approved by each member of the special manuscript committee, until forty-five days have elapsed from the transmittal of the report in manuscript form. The interval is allowed for the receipt of any memorandum of dissent or reservation, together with a brief statement of his reasons, that any member may wish to express; and such memorandum of dissent or reservation shall be published with the manuscript if he so desires. Publication does not, however, imply that each member of the Board has read the manuscript, or that either members of the Board in general or the special committee have passed on its validity in every detail.

6. Publications of the National Bureau issued for informational purposes concerning the work of the Bureau and its staff, or issued to inform the public of activities of Bureau staff, and volumes issued as a result of various conferences involving the National Bureau shall contain a specific disclaimer noting that such publication has not passed through the normal review procedures required in this resolution. The Executive Committee of the Board is charged with review of all such publications from time to time to ensure that they do not take on the character of formal research reports of the National Bureau, requiring formal Board approval.

7. Unless otherwise determined by the Board or exempted by the terms of paragraph 6, a copy of this resolution shall be printed in each National Bureau publication.

(Resolution adopted October 25, 1926, as revised through September 30, 1974)

Contents

Acknowledgments

This volume, consisting of papers presented at a conference held at Williamsburg, Virginia, 20–21 September 1984, presents research carried out within the National Bureau of Economic Research project, The Changing Roles of Debt and Equity in Financing U.S. Capital Formation. The National Bureau has undertaken this project—including the conference, the research described in this volume, and the publication of the volume itself—with the support of the American Council of Life Insurance.

The many people whose advice and assistance have helped to make this volume possible include National Bureau directors George T. Conklin, Jr., Robert C. Holland, and J. C. LaForce; National Bureau research associate Edward J. Kane; National Bureau staff members Arthur Clarke, Mark Fitz-Patrick, Kirsten Foss, Susan Ann Jannone, and Annie Spillane; and Kenneth M. Wright of the American Council of Life Insurance.

The opinions expressed in this volume are those of the respective authors. They do not necessarily reflect the views of the National Bureau of Economic Research, The American Council of Life Insurance, or any other organization.

Benjamin M. Friedman

Financing Corporate Capital Formation: An Introduction and Overview

Benjamin M. Friedman

The financing of the U.S. economy's capital formation has been a major subject of business and public policy discussion for more than a decade and a major focus of empirical inquiry by the National Bureau of Economic Research over a much longer time. Even in the 1950s and 1960s, for example, the National Bureau conducted a series of "Studies in Capital Formation and Financing," which culminated in Simon Kuznets' important volume, *Capital in the American Economy: Its Formation and Financing*. Earlier still, the National Bureau conducted a series of "Studies in Business Finance" and "Studies in Corporate Bond Financing."

This focus on the financing of capital formation is an appropriate one, no less so today than then. The central importance of capital formation to the economy's further growth and development is broadly recognized, and physical investment decisions and their financial counterparts are fundamentally interdependent. The financial environment therefore influences both the amount and the composition of the capital formation that an economy like that of the United States undertakes.

Questions about capital formation in the United States, and especially about the financing of that capital formation, inevitably focus in large part on the economy's corporate sector. Since World War II, business corporations have consistently accounted for about three-quarters of all investment in plant and equipment in the United States. The economic behavior of the corporate sector, including corporations' physical investment decisions as well as their corresponding financial decisions, constitutes a primary determinant of the economy's overall capital formation process and performance.

Benjamin M. Friedman is professor of economics at Harvard University and program director for Financial Markets and Monetary Economics at the National Bureau of Economic Research.

1

The papers in this volume summarize the principal findings of the second stage of a current, wide-ranging National Bureau effort to investigate "The Changing Roles of Debt and Equity in Financing U.S. Capital Formation." The first group of studies sponsored under this project, which were published individually and summarized in a 1982 volume bearing the same title (Friedman 1982), took a broad-based view of the evolving financial underpinnings of U.S. capital formation, addressing not only corporate sector behavior but also such issues as household saving incentives, international capital flows, and government debt management. The project's second series of studies, published together in 1985 under the title *Corporate Capital Structures in the United States* (Friedman 1985), focused more narrowly on capital formation undertaken by the U.S. corporate business sector.[1] At the same time, because corporations' securities must be held, a parallel focus in this second stage of the research was on the behavior of the markets that price the financial claims which the corporate sector issues.

The financial capital structure of an economy's business corporations, either individually or in the aggregate, is the joint product of decisions taken by claim-issuing corporations and claim-holding investors—collectively, "the market." The capital structure existing at any one time reflects the cumulative result of the entire prior history of corporate decisions on what kind of claims to issue, and how much of each, in response to the associated history of the relevant market prices. Changes in the capital structure over time therefore reflect corporate responses either to changing nonfinancial influences or to changes in the financial market environment, which in turn stem from investors' responses to a wide variety of further economic and noneconomic factors. The main goals motivating the research in the second stage of this National Bureau project was not only to advance understanding of the basic corporate-sector behavior connecting debt and equity financing to physical capital formation in the United States, but also, and more specifically, to assess how the roles of debt and equity in this process have changed over time.

Within this overall direction, three sets of questions about corporate sector and financial market behavior directly framed the research undertaken in these papers: First, what has been the actual experience of the use of debt and equity financing by U.S. business corporations in recent years? Second, what factors drive the financial markets' pricing of—that is, the setting of terms on which investors are willing to hold—debt and equity securities? And third, what is the relationship (if any) between corporations' real investment decisions and their financial decisions? Ten papers addressing these questions, written by eighteen researchers, constituted the second stage of this National Bureau project.

---

1. This introduction draws heavily on the introduction to that volume.

The papers in this volume are the authors' summaries of six of those ten papers. These six papers were prepared for a conference for corporate and financial sector practitioners that the National Bureau sponsored at Williamsburg, Virginia, on September 20–21, 1984. The conference itself provided an opportunity for the participating researchers to report their findings to, and receive valuable feedback from, an audience consisting of senior corporate sector financial executives and senior executives of financial firms. The six papers presented at that conference, and published here for the first time, provide an overview of the second stage of this National Bureau project, which is now complete.

The first three of the ten papers comprising this stage of the project established the basic empirical facts of the changes that have (and, in some cases, have not) taken place in U.S. corporate capital structures and in the financial price and yield relationships that U.S. corporations have faced in recent years.

Robert A. Taggart's paper, "Secular Patterns in Corporate Finance," set the stage for the entire series of studies by first developing a conceptual framework for thinking about changes in corporate capital structures and then assembling and analyzing relevant time series data going back in many cases to the beginning of the twentieth century. Taggart began by using available aggregate time series data to document the main features of the changes that have occurred over time. He showed that the use of debt by U.S. corporations has increased considerably since World War II, as is familiar, but also that current debt levels are not necessarily high by prewar standards. The postwar surge in corporate debt certainly appears less dramatic when viewed in the context of the whole century's experience. Taggart also documented several other changes that have occurred, including the increasing importance of short-term relative to long-term debt, and the declining importance of new issues of either common or preferred stock relative to internally generated equity.

In his paper's more theoretical sections, Taggart reviewed several basic explanations of the determination of firm and/or aggregate corporate capital structures, including those relying on the trade-off between bankruptcy costs and tax savings from deductibility of interest payments, on the relative agency costs of debt and equity, on problems of providing relevant information to security holders, and on the differential between personal and corporate tax rates. Taggart laid out the relationships among these four separate approaches and used them to examine a series of potential influences on corporate capital structures including tax factors, price inflation, supplies of competing securities, and the physical characteristics of corporate investment.

Taggart then went on to ask which among these different explanations could plausibly account for the main changes that have taken place. He concluded that tax factors in conjunction with inflation have played an important role, but nevertheless not one sufficient to explain the chief trends that have occurred over long periods of time. He argued that, in addition, supplies of competing securities like government bonds, along with the secular development of the nation's financial intermediary system, may also be important determinants of long-run corporate financing patterns.

Taggart's paper, "Have U.S. Corporations Grown Financially Weak?", which appears as Chapter 1 of this volume, summarizes the chief findings of this extensive work.

John H. Ciccolo and Christopher F. Baum's paper, "Changes in the Balance Sheet of the U.S. Manufacturing Sector, 1926–1977," took a closer look at an important slice of the corporate sector's capital structure on the basis of a new data series developed as part of this National Bureau project and now available to other researchers. Ciccolo and Baum developed a new data series for a rolling sample of approximately 50 manufacturing firms, spanning a half-century and including for each firm a large number of balance sheet and income account items. A major contribution of this data set is the ready availability, for the first time, of accurate information on the market value of corporations' publicly traded liabilities. In addition, the data set Ciccolo and Baum developed provides estimates of the replacement value of firms' physical assets, as well as computations of rates of return based on both market and replacement values.

Ciccolo and Baum showed that the chief aggregate features exhibited by this data set over time are broadly consistent with the principal developments documented at the aggregate level by other researchers. The data show an increasing importance of external funds, and especially of debt, in financing corporations' physical capital formation. On the asset side, the data show a substantial decline in corporations' holdings of cash and short-term marketable securities. Rates of return have declined on balance within the post–World War II period, but not from the perspective of a longer time frame. In the latter half of the postwar period, market valuations of corporations' net assets have declined dramatically in relation either to replacement values or to realized rates of return.

As an illustration of its potential applications, Ciccolo and Baum used the 1927–35 and 1966–77 panels of their data set to examine the relationship of movements of corporations' key balance sheet items to changes in their net cash flow and to changes in the ratio of market to replacement value of their net assets. The principal idea at issue here is that firms face different constraints, and therefore behave differently, when they are attempting to increase their stock of physical capital than when they are trying to reduce it. The empirical results that Ciccolo and Baum found generally support this kind of relationship for the later (more normal) period, but not for the earlier one dominated by the Depression.

Patric H. Hendershott and Roger D. Huang's paper, "Debt and Equity Yields, 1926–1980," provided a parallel review and analysis of the market prices and yields that U.S. corporations have faced in deciding on their capital structures. Hendershott and Huang first documented the principal movements of and interrelationships among debt and equity yields in the United States over a half-century, including both secular and cyclical movements. They then went on to test several familiar propositions about these yield relationships.

Hendershott and Huang focused in the first instance on corporate bond and equity yields, the market prices most directly relevant to capital structure decisions, but for purposes of analysis and comparison their work also included the yields on both short- and long-term U.S. Treasury securities. A familiar result, which their review of the experience of these yields reinforced, is the contrast between the patterns that have dominated the post–World War II period and the events of the 1930s. A less familiar result, which emerged strongly in their work nevertheless, is the appearance of strong regularities in security yield movements over the business cycle, including systematic differences in the cyclical movements of ex post returns on bonds and equities. The strength of equity returns during the year surrounding business cycle troughs stands out especially clearly.

Hendershott and Huang also investigated several familiar hypotheses about the determination of debt and equity yields. The principal conclusion of their work here is that unanticipated price inflation, which they represented by the difference between the actual inflation experience and the corresponding estimate in the Livingston survey, is a major determinant of these yields. Other factors also emerged from their analysis as bearing on the determination of yields, however—including, in particular, measures of real economic activity like industrial production and capacity utilization.

Hendershott's paper, "Debt and Equity Returns Revisited," which appears as Chapter 2 of this volume, summarizes and extends this work.

Against the background of this general review of the experience of both the quantities and the prices associated with changes in corporate capital structures in the United States, the next four papers addressed more directly the market mechanism determining the prices and yields on debt and equity securities. Of these four, the first two focused on more general aspects of the behavior of investors in debt and equity securities, while the next two examined the market pricing mechanism in contexts more specifically related to actual or potential changes in corporate capital structures.

Zvi Bodie, Alex Kane, and Robert McDonald's paper, "Inflation and the Role of Bonds in Investor Portfolios," explored both theoretically and empirically the role of nominal (that is, not indexed) bonds of various maturities in the portfolios of U.S. investors. A principal goal of their analysis was to determine whether an investor constrained to hold bonds only in the form of a single portfolio of nominal debt instruments—as is the case, for example, in employer-sponsored saving plans offering a choice between a common stock fund and a single bond fund—will suffer a serious welfare loss. For this purpose Bodie and his colleagues took as their measure of welfare gain or loss, due to a given change in the investor's opportunity set, the increment to the investor's current wealth needed to offset that change. A second goal of their analysis was to study the desirability and feasibility of introducing a market for indexed bonds, offering a riskless real return, in the United States.

Bodie and his colleagues used the risk structure of real returns computed from historical data for 1953–81, in combination with assumptions about net asset supplies and about investors' average degree of risk aversion, to derive estimates of the risk premia on the various assets they studied. From this procedure they concluded that a substantial loss in welfare can be associated with participation in a savings plan offering a choice only between a diversified common stock fund and an intermediate-term bond fund. They argued that it is possible to eliminate most of this loss, however, by introducing, as a third option in such plans, a fund consisting of short-term money market instruments. Bodie et al. also concluded that the potential welfare gain from introducing explicitly indexed bonds in the U.S. financial market is probably not large enough to justify the costs of innovation by private issuers. The major reason the gain would be so small is that 1-month U.S. Treasury bills, with their small variance of real returns, already constitute an effective substitute for indexed bonds in investors' portfolios.

"Risk and Required Returns on Debt and Equity," which appears as Chapter 3 of this volume, summarizes this work by Bodie et al. and applies it to help explain why real interest rates have been so high in recent years in the United States. Their principal conclusion is that the increased volatility of bond prices since the 1979 change in the Federal Reserve System's operating procedures has substantially increased the required risk premium on long-term bonds. By contrast, they consider but reject the possibility that increased risk alone accounts for the recent high level of U.S. short-term interest rates.

My own paper, "The Substitutability of Debt and Equity Securities," investigated empirically the degree to which investors in U.S. markets consider debt and equity as substitutes in their portfolios—an aspect of investors' behavior that has an important influence on, among other matters, whether government deficits "crowd out" private financing and private capital formation. The analysis first applied fundamental relationships connecting portfolio choices with expected asset returns to infer key asset substitutabilities directly from the risk structure of U.S. asset returns during 1960–80. It then compared these implied substitutabilities with corresponding estimates obtained from data on the actual portfolio behavior of U.S. households.

The resulting evidence provided little ground for any conclusion about even the sign, much less the magnitude, of the substitutability of short-term debt and equity. Although the risk structure indicated that these two assets are substitutes, observed household portfolio behavior indicated that investors have treated them as complements. By contrast, the evidence consistently indicated that *long-term* debt and equity are substitutes, albeit with a small degree of substitutability. This analysis therefore bears mixed implications for broader substantive economic and financial questions.

My paper, "Implications of Government Deficits for Interest Rates, Equity Returns and Corporate Financing," which appears as Chapter 4 of this volume, summarizes parts of this work and applies it to consider the crowding-out question explicitly. The results indicate that government financing raises expected debt returns relative to expected equity returns, regardless of the maturity of the government's financing. Continuing large government deficits at full employment therefore lead to market incentives for individual business corporations to emphasize reliance on equity (including retentions), and reduce reliance on debt, in comparison with the composition of corporate financing that would prevail in the absence of the need to finance the government's deficit.

Wayne H. Mikkelson's paper, "Capital Structure Change and Decreases in Stockholders' Wealth: A Cross-sectional Study of Convertible Security Calls," examined the financial markets' pricing of corporate securities in the specific context of the changes in common stock values that occur when firms call outstanding convertible debt or preferred stock. Mikkelson's goals were to investigate the potential determinants of the usually observed negative common stock price reaction to the announcement of a convertible security call forcing conversion and, on the basis of this analysis, to draw inferences about the pricing of corporate securities and hence about the determination of corporate capital structures more generally.

Mikkelson's empirical work related the observed changes in common stock prices following 164 convertible security calls made by U.S. corporations during 1962–78 to several quantifiable effects associated with these calls—including the change in interest expense tax shields, the potential redistribution of wealth from common stockholders to holders of debt or preferred stock, the decrease in value of the conversion option held by owners of the convertible securities, the increase in the number of common shares outstanding, and the change in earnings per share. Among these various effects, only the reduction in interest expense tax shields exhibited a significant relationship to the change in common stock price.

Mikkelson argued that this result is consistent with systematic reductions in common stock prices due not only to reductions in interest expense tax shields, as would be implied by theories relating optimal capital structure to tax factors, but also to the negative information about corporations' earnings prospects conveyed by convertible security calls. He therefore concluded that this evidence is also consistent with theories which relate a corporation's capital structure to its earnings prospects, and hence which imply that a reduction in leverage conveys unfavorable information about the corporation's value.

E. Philip Jones, Scott P. Mason, and Eric Rosenfeld's paper, "Contingent Claims Valuation of Corporate Liabilities: Theory and Empirical Tests," addressed the specific question of how the financial markets value the complicated securities, encumbered by numerous covenants and indenture provisions, that U.S. corporations typically issue. The central tool in their analysis is the familiar contingent claims model, which applies to the pricing of corporate liabilities the fundamental insight that every corporate security is a contingent claim on the value of the underlying firm. Hence it is possible to model the financial markets' pricing of these securities via an arbitrage logic that is independent of other, less straightforward aspects of the structure of risk and return. Under this useful model, the price of every security depends in a formally quantifiable way on the rate of return on riskless assets and on the issuing firm's market value and the volatility of that value.

Jones and his colleagues laid out the basic contingent claims model, extended it to cover such practically relevant special cases as multiple debt issues of a single firm and debt issues with sinking funds (with and without an option to double the associated payment schedule), and then tested the expanded model using monthly 1975–82 data on the actual market prices of 177 bonds issued by 15 U.S. corporations. They concluded that their empirical results do not warrant using the model, in its conventional form, as a practical basis for valuing corporate securities. Although there is almost no systematic bias in the pricing errors that the model makes for the sample as a whole, the model does systematically over- or underprice bonds with specific characteristics. In particular, the model tends to *underprice* less risky bonds and *overprice* more risky bonds. This failure led Jones and his colleagues to suggest that several of the standard assumptions underlying contingent claims analysis in its usual form are inconsistent with the actual workings of the U.S. financial markets.

Mason's paper, "Valuing Financial Flexibility," which appears as Chapter 5 of this volume, summarizes this work and extends it to demonstrate the impact of changing interest rate volatility on the value of call provisions and call protection.

The last three papers in this second stage of the research returned to a more direct focus on the observed capital structures of U.S. corporations, now emphasizing in particular the question of the relationship (if any) of capital structure decisions to corporations' real-sector behavior.

Michael S. Long and Ileen S. Malitz's paper, "Investment Patterns and Financial Leverage," focused on one of the major elements underlying familiar theories of corporate capital structures: the role of investment opportunities. An important implication of such models is that corporations' real and financial decisions are connected. In this case the connection takes the form of a systematic bias toward underinvestment when firms with risky debt outstanding act in the interest of their shareholders. One potential role of complex covenants in debt contracts is to alleviate this problem.

Long and Malitz argued that, because growth opportunities that are firm-specific and intangible (and hence unobservable) reduce the effectiveness of debt covenants, corporations with a high proportion of their investment opportunities in intangible form can limit the agency costs imposed on holders of their debt only by limiting the amount of risky debt they have outstanding. Conversely, by using appropriately structured debt covenants, corporations with a high proportion of their investment opportunities in the form of tangible assets like capital equipment can reduce these costs and therefore can support a greater level of debt. Hence a key determinant of the corporation's optimal capital structure is the specific type of investment opportunity it faces.

Long and Malitz presented empirical results, based on 1978–80 data for a sample of 545 U.S. corporations, that provide evidence in support of such a relationship between real and financial corporate behavior. In particular, their results show that corporations that invest heavily in intangibles—research and development, for example, or advertising—systematically rely less on debt than do corporations that invest largely in tangibles. These results also stand up in the presence of other variables like tax factors that represent alternative explanations of capital structure decisions, although there is evidence that the most important single determinant of corporations' borrowing decisions remains the availability of internal funds.

Michael Spence's paper, "Capital Structure and the Corporation's Product Market Environment," examined the potential relationship between corporations' real and financial behavior from a different perspective. Spence argued that, if choosing an optimal capital structure is a way for a corporation to reduce its costs in some relevant sense, then corporations facing greater competitive pressure in their product markets will have a greater incentive, and hence a greater tendency, to do so than will corporations enjoying more sheltered competitive environments. Alternatively, if theories treating financial structure as irrelevant are correct, then there would be no observed connection between competitive product markets and observed patterns of corporate capital structures.

Spence tested this hypothesis by relating the observed interfirm variance of capital structures to measures of product market competitive pressure for 1183 U.S. corporations in 403 four-digit industries. His measures of competitiveness included returns earned by firms as well as variables directly and indirectly reflecting entry barriers and potential oligopolistic consensus. Spence also included in the empirical work measures of product market diversification for each firm, so as to be able to distinguish the behavior of the full sample from the behavior of a smaller sample of relatively undiversified firms.

Spence found that, although industry product market environments help explain the returns that firms earn and also bear systematic relationships to firms' actual capital structures, they apparently do not much influence intra-industry deviations of firms' capital structures from the respective implied industry optima. One possible explanation for this negative result, of course, is that capital structure does not strongly influence corporations' costs, or hence their total value—in other words, that there exists no optimal capital structure. The positive results that emerged from Spence's analysis seem inconsistent with this view, however. An alternative explanation is that, while optimal capital structures do exist, the factors which give rise to them simply do not become significantly more influential in more competitive environments.

Finally, Alan J. Auerbach's paper, "Real Determinants of Corporate Leverage," focused on still another of the key factors underlying several familiar theories of optimal corporate capital structures: the role of taxes. Here again, what makes such models especially interesting is that corporations' real and financial decisions are connected. In particular, Auerbach argued that the U.S. corporate income tax distorts corporations' real-sector behavior, via the variation in depreciation allowances and investment tax credit provisions across different types of physical investments, and also distorts financial behavior via the differential treatment of debt and equity returns. The object of his analysis of corporations' real and financial decisions was to determine the extent to which these biases offset one another.

Auerbach's analysis began from the basic idea that corporations prefer to finance different physical investments in different ways. Such behavior would be important in this context because the conclusion that tax effects bias investment choices is necessarily valid only if there is a separation between real and financial decisions. For example, if a corporation's optimal capital structure depends on a tax advantage to debt financing which is dissipated by risk-related costs as the firm's leverage increases, and if these risk-related costs in turn depend on the corporation's investment mix, then the resulting *financial* bias in favor of investing in structures could offset the initial *tax* bias in favor of investing in equipment.

Auerbach's empirical work, based on 1958–77 data for a panel of 189 U.S. corporations, suggested that observed patterns of real and financial behavior are only partially consistent with familiar theories of optimal capital structure based on tax factors and on costs connected to agency considerations and risks of bankruptcy. The effect of corporations' growth rates on their borrowing is inconsistent with the predictions of models based on agency costs. In addition, although the effect of the tax loss carry-forward is consistent with models based on tax shields, the effect of earnings variance is not. Auerbach also concluded that there is no obvious financial offset to the tax bias against investment in structures, since, on the whole, corporations do not appear to borrow more to invest in structures than in equipment.

Auerbach's paper, "The Economic Effects of the Corporate Income Tax: Changing Revenues and Changing Views," which appears as Chapter 6 of this volume, summarizes and extends this analysis.

References

Friedman, B. M. ed. 1982. *The Changing Roles of Debt and Equity in Financing U.S. Capital Formation.* Chicago: University of Chicago Press (for NBER).

Friedman, B. M. ed. 1985. *Corporate Capital Structures in the United States.* Chicago: University of Chicago Press (for NBER).

1 Have U.S. Corporations Grown Financially Weak?

Robert A. Taggart, Jr.

The feeling is widespread that the financial strength of U.S. corporations has eroded over the past 20 years.[1] The apparent increase in debt financing, especially short-term and floating rate debt, has alarmed many observers. Declining liquidity ratios and heavy reliance on external funds have also caused concern. These trends typically are blamed on some combination of three factors: the tax system, which is said to favor debt over equity financing: inflation, which causes internal funds to lag behind total needs and is alleged to make debt cheap; and overly optimistic assessments of business risk.

This paper examines corporate financing developments of the past two decades from a long-run perspective. Recent years' trends are compared with those for the twentieth century as a whole in an attempt to shed some light on the following questions: Is it true that corporations have increasingly relied on external funds of all kinds, especially debt? Are the trends of recent years unusual in light of prior years? What causes long-run patterns in corporate finance? Have U.S. corporations indeed become financially weak?

Section 1.1 of the paper uses a variety of data sources to determine what financing trends have actually occurred over the twentieth century. Special emphasis is placed on the problem of accurate measurement during

Robert A. Taggart, Jr., is professor of finance at Boston University and a research associate of the National Bureau of Economic Research. This chapter draws in large part on the research reported in Taggart 1985.

1. This feeling is especially prevalent among members of the business press (see *Business Week* 1974, 1982; Carson-Parker 1981; Bennett 1984) and analysts of the financial system (see Massaro 1977; Mains 1980; Kaufman 1981; Moran 1984). Government officials have also expressed concern over corporate financing trends, particularly in the wake of the leveraged buyout boom (e.g., Shad 1984).

inflationary periods. Section 1.2 examines the ability of taxes, inflation, and perceived business risk to explain these financing trends. The impact of federal government borrowing on the financing decisions of the business sector is also considered. Section 1.3 summarizes the paper's findings and attempts to identify the key determinants of future developments in corporate financing.

1.1   Corporate Financing Trends, 1900–1983

1.1.1   Debt Ratios

Perhaps the most commonly used measure of financial condition is some form of debt ratio, computed with ordinary accounting data. For the U.S. corporate sector as a whole, such data are available from the Internal Revenue Service *Statistics of Income* for the years 1926–81, and from these data the ratio of long-term debt to total capitalization is graphed in figure 1.1. It is easy to see from this figure why there is a widespread feeling not only that corporate debt usage has increased steadily in the years since World War II but that it has reached historical peaks in recent years.[2] Perhaps less widely appreciated is the apparent fact that the rise in debt ratios ceased in the early 1970s. One might conclude from figure 1.1 that U.S. corporations were increasingly willing to take on financial risk in the postwar years but that debt ratios have remained stable at a new higher plateau for roughly the past decade.

However, the accounting data on which figure 1.1 is based are subject to several potential biases and should be interpreted with caution. Liberalization of depreciation allowances, as has occurred at several points from the 1960s onward, increases corporate cash flow but reduces measured profits and retained earnings. Thus debt ratios will tend to be overstated when allowed depreciation is increased. Inflation also causes distortions in accounting data. Reported asset values may be understated in an inflation, resulting in overstated debt ratios. Likewise, standard accounting data do not reflect decreases in the real value of debt, and reported debt ratios may thus exaggerate the real burden of corporate liabilities. On the other hand, accounting data have not traditionally included such off-balance-sheet items as lease obligations and unfunded pension liabilities, so reported debt ratios may also contain some understatements.[3]

---

2. Perceived trends, of course, are always dependent on the observer's reference point. Miller (1963) examined the same data from 1926 through the mid-1950s and concluded, quite reasonably, that there had been no trend in corporate debt ratios over this period.

3. Gordon and Malkiel (1981) present evidence for the period 1973–78 suggesting that inclusion of lease and pension obligations would increase reported debt ratios by approximately one-third.

FRACTION OF
TOTAL CAPITALIZATION

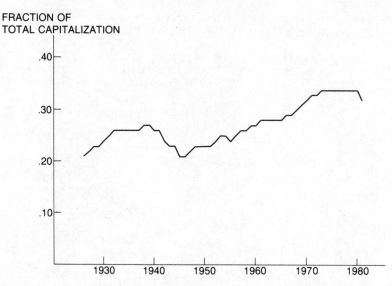

Fig. 1.1   Ratio of long-term debt to total capitalization, all United
States corporations

Figure 1.2 tracks the movement of two alternative debt ratio calculations that attempt to correct for some of the biases in standard accounting
data. The first of these is an estimated ratio of the market value of debt to
the market value of total capitalization of U.S. nonfinancial corporations. The underlying data are taken from Holland and Myers (1979),
who estimated market values for debt and equity by capitalizing total corporate interest and dividend payments at current market yields. The market value ratio should adjust for inflation-induced valuation changes and
thus provide a more accurate measure of the burden of corporate debt.
The primary disadvantages of this measure are that it is subject to estimation error, and it does not allow separation of actual corporate financing
decisions from changes in market valuation.

As shown in figure 1.2, the market value debt ratio is more volatile than
the book value ratio. It does, however, exhibit somewhat the same general
pattern. Corporate debt ratios were relatively high in the 1930s and early
1940s, but they declined markedly by the end of World War II. There then
appears to have been an upward trend in the postwar period, although the
market value data suggest that much of the upward movement took place
in the late 1960s and early 1970s. Finally, this rise in the debt ratio leveled
off in the mid-1970s, with declines occurring in the most recent years.

The second ratio graphed in figure 1.2 is an estimated ratio of the market value of debt to the replacement value of assets for U.S. nonfinancial

FRACTION OF TOTAL ASSETS,
FRACTION OF TOTAL CAPITALIZATION

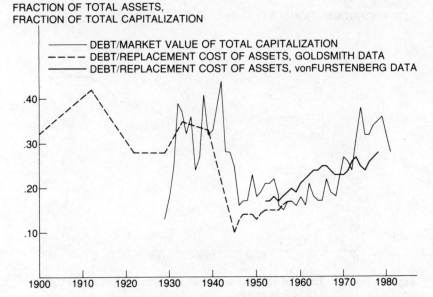

Fig. 1.2   Market value and replacement value debt ratios, United States
                  nonfinancial corporations

corporations. Like the market value data, the replacement value estimates
are aimed at eliminating inflationary distortions. Another advantage of
this measure is that by combining the estimates of Goldsmith et al. (1963)
for the early years with more recent estimates by von Furstenberg (1977),
it is possible to put together a long series of comparable ratios.

Again, the replacement value ratios exhibit a broad pattern that is similar in many respects to that of the book value ratios: corporate debt usage
apparently fell to a low point at the end of World War II and subsequently
rose. However, the replacement value data suggest that the steadiest increases were over by the mid-1960s, with a more cyclical pattern ensuing
since then. An especially interesting feature of the replacement value data
is their implication that corporate debt usage was quite high early in the
century. By these estimates, the corporate debt ratio was unusually low at
the end of World War II, and it has only recently attained the levels that
were normal in the period 1900–1930.

Considered as a group, all three debt ratio measures suggest that the
end of World War II may be a quite misleading reference point from
which to judge recent corporate financing trends. It seems undeniable that
corporate debt usage has risen in the postwar period, but it is far from
clear that current debt levels are unusually high when viewed from a long-
run perspective.

1.1.2   Liquidity Ratios

Liquidity ratios are a second type of balance sheet ratio frequently used to measure financial condition. The ratios of liquid assets to total assets and to short-term liabilities for U.S. nonfinancial corporations are shown in table 1.1 for selected years. Total assets are measured at replacement value, while short-term liabilities are measured at book value.

As worried observers have noted, there indeed appears to have been a substantial decline in corporate liquidity during the postwar period. However, as with the debt ratios, 1945 was a year of unusually low financial risk for corporations. Not only were their debt ratios at historic lows by the end of the war, but they held large amounts of U.S. government securities as well. If we subtracted liquid asset holdings from total debt, we would see that corporations were effectively in a position of negative leverage at that time.

From a longer-run perspective, recent ratios of liquid assets to total assets do not seem alarmingly low. Their levels are roughly commensurate with those of the 1900–1930 period. It does appear, though, that the most recent ratio of liquid assets to short-term liabilities is somewhat low, even by historical standards. This suggests that short-term debt has risen in relative terms at the same time that liquid assets have been declining. Whether or not this trend is cause for concern will be considered further below.

Table 1.1   Liquid Asset Ratios, U.S. Nonfinancial Corporations

Year	Liquid Assets* Total Assets	Liquid Assets† Short-Term Liabilities
1900	.061	.299
1912	.066	.322
1922	.070	.300
1929	.067	.311
1933	.060	.297
1939	.076	.452
1945	.167	.822
1953	.121	.597
1964	.086	.373
1975	.056	.301
1982	N.A.	.248

*Liquid assets consist of currency, deposits, and marketable securities other than corporate stock. Total assets are measured at replacement value. Data for 1900–1945 are from Goldsmith et al. (1963) and for 1953–75 from Goldsmith (1982).

†Short-term liabilities are loans (except mortgages), short-term paper, profit taxes payable, and trade debt. Data for 1900–1945 are from Goldsmith et al. (1963) and for 1953–82 from Board of Governors of the Federal Reserve System, Flow of Funds Accounts.

1.1.3 Flows of Funds

A different approach to assessing corporations' financial condition is to examine flows of funds over selected periods. While the balance sheet measures the cumulative effect of all prior flows as of a particular moment, the flow data reflect corporations' actual financing decisions during specified periods. In figure 1.3, for example, the yearly flows of gross internal funds (retained earnings plus depreciation allowances), total debt, and new equity issues, expressed as fractions of total yearly sources of funds for U.S. nonfinancial corporations, are graphed for the period

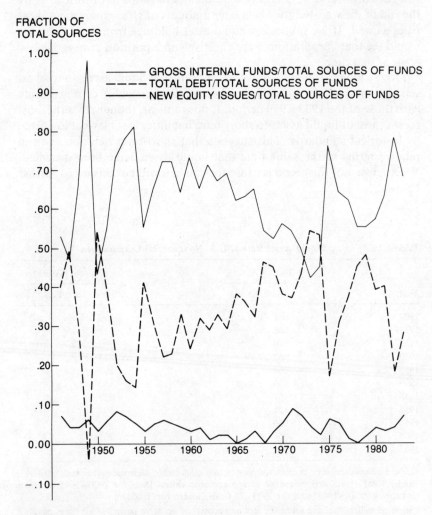

Fig. 1.3   Composition of funds sources, United States nonfinancial corporations

1946–83. Data are taken from the Federal Reserve's Flow of Funds Accounts.

These data do give one indication of financial duress for the corporate sector in recent years that was not readily apparent in the balance sheet data: the volatility of funds flow composition has increased tremendously since the early 1970s. The availability of internal funds relative to total financing needs has alternately plunged and soared. Simultaneously, debt usage has reached unusually high levels when internal funds were short and unusually low levels when internal funds were plentiful. Once again it should be noted, though, that one's reference point is important to any conclusions about volatility. It could possibly be argued that the period from the late 1950s to the late 1960s was one of unusual stability and that recent fluctuations are more akin to those experienced in the immediate postwar years.

An accurate picture of long-term trends is more likely to emerge if we smooth out some of these yearly fluctuations. The same funds flow ratios are thus shown for 5-year periods in table 1.2. The use of longer periods also allows the Federal Reserve Flow of Funds data to be supplemented by

Table 1.2   **Composition of Financing Flows, U.S. Nonfinancial Corporations**

				Fractions of Total Sources of Funds*		
Period	Total Debt (1)	Long-Term Debt† (2)	Total Short-Term Liabilities (3)	Short-Term Credit Market Debt‡ (4)	New Stock Issues (5)	Gross Internal Funds (6)
1901–12	.31	.23	.08		.14	.55
1913–22	.29	.12	.17		.11	.60
1923–29	.26	.22	.04		.19	.55
1930–39	−.33	−.05	−.29		.19	1.14
1940–45	.15	−.05	.20		.05	.80
1946–48	.40	.18	.22	.09	.04	.56
1949–53	.30	.14	.16	.04	.06	.64
1954–58	.28	.15	.13	.05	.05	.68
1959–63	.30	.14	.16	.06	.02	.68
1964–68	.37	.15	.22	.10	.01	.62
1969–73	.45	.19	.26	.11	.06	.50
1974–78	.38	.13	.25	.12	.02	.60
1979–83	.35	.09	.26	.14	.02	.63

*Columns may not add to totals because of rounding.
†Long-term debt is defined as bonds and mortgages. All bank loans are included as short-term debt even though some fraction of these have maturities longer than one year.
‡Includes bank loans, commercial paper, acceptances, finance company loans and U.S. government loans.
Sources: Goldsmith (1958) and Board of Governors of the Federal Reserve System, Flow of Funds Accounts.

Goldsmith's (1958) estimates of funds flow composition for selected periods between 1900 and 1945.

Several trends are apparent in table 1.2. First, debt has accounted for a consistently larger fraction of total financing since the mid-1960s than was the case for nearly all prior periods. Even with recent declines from the 1969–73 peak, debt financing appears to be quite high. Second, the rise in debt financing has not been caused by an increase in long-term debt, which, if anything, may exhibit some downtrend. Rather, it is short-term liabilities that have increased markedly. Third, the increase in short-term debt cannot be predominantly attributed to the growth of such spontaneous liabilities as tax accruals and trade debt. Much of it has come from credit market instruments, such as bank loans and commercial paper.[4] Fourth, stock issues fell precipitously as a source of funds during World War II and have remained low ever since. Finally, it is difficult to discern any long-run trend in internal funds.

At least in part, then, any trend toward increased debt-equity ratios could be characterized as a substitution of short-term debt for external equity. Such a characterization offers some support for the fears of those observers who argue that U.S. corporations have dramatically increased their exposure to financial risk.

However, this interpretation of the data is subject to qualification. As it does with the balance sheet ratios, inflation may distort the financing picture reflected in the Flow of Funds data. In particular, von Furstenberg and Malkiel (1977) have argued that annual funds flows should be adjusted for any changes in firms' real indebtedness during the year that are caused by changes in the price level.

Suppose, for example, that the real interest rate is 4%. If expected inflation suddenly increases from zero to 8%, lenders will demand a nominal interest rate of roughly 12% in order to provide themselves a 4% real return. If the inflationary process is neutral, one would expect these nominal adjustments to take place, leaving the real pattern of corporate profits, investment, and financing undisturbed.

Note, however, that in this example a neutral inflation will increase corporations' operating cash flows by 8%, while their nominal interest payments rise by 200%. As conventionally reported, corporate internal funds will not rise as fast as the inflation rate. If the flow of debt financing remains constant in real terms, this necessarily implies that nominal debt financing will rise relative to nominal internal funds.

4. Some portion of bank loans should in fact be classified as longterm, but the actual fraction is impossible to estimate with any degree of confidence. There is no evidence of any trend toward increasingly long-term bank loans from, say, the mid-1960s onward. Moreover, the predominance of floating rate loans in recent years implies that even bank term loans have many of the characteristics of short-term debt.

The inflation premium in nominal interest payments is more appropriately treated as a return of the lender's real principal, which just compensates for the decline in real value of the nominal principal. As a return of principal, however, this amount should not be deducted from corporate profits but rather treated as any other net retirement of debt. By this argument, we should therefore add to reported internal funds any decline in the real value of outstanding debt, since it is not in the true sense a current expense. The same amount should also be subtracted from reported debt issues. Since it represents a retirement of real principal, only new debt issues over and above this amount represent net increases in real debt.

The data in table 1.2 were therefore adjusted for changes in real indebtedness, following the procedure outlined in von Furstenberg and Malkiel (1977). The revised relative proportions of gross internal funds and total debt are shown in table 1.3, alongside the corresponding unadjusted figures.

Table 1.3   **Composition of Corporate Financing Flows Adjusted for Changes in Real Indebtedness**

| | Fractions of Total Sources | | | |
| | Gross Internal Funds | | Total Debt | |
Period	Unadjusted* (1)	Adjusted† (2)	Unadjusted (3)	Adjusted (4)
1901–12	.55	.56	.31	.30
1913–22	.60	.67	.29	.22
1923–29	.55	.55	.26	.26
1930–39	1.14	1.23	−.33	−.39
1940–45	.80	.87	.15	.08
1946–48	.56	.64	.40	.32
1949–53	.64	.67	.30	.27
1954–58	.68	.71	.28	.24
1959–63	.68	.69	.30	.29
1964–68	.62	.65	.37	.34
1969–73	.50	.56	.45	.39
1974–78	.60	.71	.38	.27
1979–83	.63	.75	.35	.23

*Unadjusted financing flow data are from Goldsmith (1958) and Board of Governors of the Federal Reserve System, Flow of Funds Accounts.

†Data are adjusted by subtracting the change in real indebtedness for the period from gross internal funds and adding the same change to total debt. Changes in price level are measured by the implicit GNP deflator for 1901–48 (source: *Historical Statistics of the United States*) and by the index of total cost and profit for nonfinancial corporations for 1949–83 (source: *Economic Report of the President*). Data on total liabilities outstanding at the beginning of each period are from Goldsmith et al. (1963) and Board of Governors of the Federal Reserve System, Flow of Funds Accounts.

The adjusted figures give the impression that recent debt proportions are by no means unusually high. Even after adjusting for inflation, however, the proportions of debt financing in the late 1960s and early 1970s were unusually high, and the past 8 years have witnessed a substantial correction. Much of this correction has occurred through heavy reliance on adjusted internal sources. Instead of financing funds needs with increasing or even constant proportions of real debt, corporations have in effect been retiring some of their maturing real debt principal with internal funds.

1.1.4   Dividend Payout Ratios

The assertion that corporations have placed heavy emphasis on internal funds in recent years naturally raises the question whether they have sacrificed dividend payments in order to do so. Three measures of corporate dividend payout over selected periods are presented in table 1.4.

The ratios in columns 1 and 2 measure dividend payments relative to total available internal funds. Both the adjusted and unadjusted internal funds measures from table 1.3 have been used in computing these ratios. The data suggest that corporations did indeed cut their dividend payout somewhat, even before the peak in debt issuance, in an attempt to increase the share of equity financing.

Table 1.4   **Dividend Payout Ratios**

	Dividends		Dividends
	Dividends Plus Gross Internal Funds		Net Profit after Tax
	U.S. Nonfinancial Corporations		
Period	Unadjusted (1)	Adjusted (2)	All U.S. Corporations (3)
1922–23			.64
1924–28			.74
1929–33			1.40
1934–38			1.30
1939–43			.65
1944–48			.46
1949–53	.27	.27	.53
1954–58	.26	.25	.60
1959–63	.24	.24	.67
1964–68	.24	.22	.50
1969–73	.23	.21	.54
1974–78	.22	.19	.39
1979–83	.23	.20	.55

Sources: Board of Governors of the Federal Reserve System, Flow of Funds Accounts, and U.S. Internal Revenue Service, *Statistics of Income*

The more traditional measure of payout, dividends divided by net profit after taxes, is shown in column 3. These figures also convey the impression that dividends were cut fairly severely in order to conserve internal funds, beginning as early as the mid-1960s. Some of the decline in payout in the mid-1960s may be attributable to the well-known tendency of dividends to lag behind profits. However, subsequent periods were not particularly profitable ones for U.S. corporations, so this does not explain away the long period of relatively low payouts from 1964 to the present. The decline in payout during the 1974–78 period is particularly dramatic.

1.1.5   Summary of Financing Trends

Does the weight of the evidence support the view that U.S. corporations have become increasingly prone to financial weakness? In most respects, I believe the most plausible answer is no. Many assertions of corporate balance sheet deterioration use the end of World War II as their reference point, but as we have seen, that was hardly a typical time. Viewed from a longer-run perspective, current corporate debt usage does not appear dangerously high nor does liquidity appear dangerously low.[5] In addition, adjustment for inflationary distortions over the past 15 years removes some of the trend toward increased debt that appears in the raw data. Finally, it should be recognized that corporations have made substantial efforts over the past 8 years, particularly through reduced dividend payout, to rebuild financial strength.

Nevertheless, some opposing points must be conceded. The financial environment of the past 10–15 years has been more volatile, as is reflected in the sharp changes in the composition of funds sources. Corporate treasurers have had to act more nimbly and imaginatively in order to keep up with the fluctuations in external funds needs. Increased use of short-term and floating rate debt has undeniably made corporations more vulnerable to interest rate fluctuations. And even if some of corporate borrowing in recent years is a rolling over of real principal instead of net new debt, it is still true that these rollovers necessitate more frequent visits to the capital market.

1.2   What Causes the Trends in Corporate Financing?

Regardless of our perception of financial strength or weakness, we could feel more comfortable with our understanding of these corporate financing developments if we knew their primary determinants. This in turn necessitates a theory of corporate capital structure.

---

5. See also Mitchell (1983) for an elaboration of the argument that, even if liquidity ratios have declined, the growth of bank loan commitments and the commercial paper market have increased corporations' ability to raise funds on short notice.

It is widely believed that corporations adjust their financing to some target balance sheet composition. As Myers (1984) has argued, the adjustment process may be quite slow, and thus there may be a good deal of slippage between actual and target balance sheets. For example, subject to their established dividend policies, firms may have a decided preference for internal over external funds and, to the extent that external funds are needed, for debt over stock issues. Thus when internal funds are plentiful relative to investment needs, debt ratios will fall below target, while the reverse will occur when internal funds are in short supply.

Despite this slippage, the influence of the target financing composition will be felt over the long run. Corporations do reach points where they feel their debt capacity is exhausted and they must turn to external equity. Moreover, the standards for debt capacity and the willingness to issue equity appear to change over time. From table 1.2, the reluctance to issue equity was apparently much less in the 1900–1940 period than it has been in recent decades.

The primary determinants of these changing standards that have been emphasized by business financing observers are perceptions of business risk, the level of corporate and personal taxes, and inflation. In the paragraphs that follow I will explore the extent to which changes in these underlying factors correspond to business financing patterns. The possible influence of federal government borrowing on business financing will also be considered.

1.2.1 Business Risk

Since the threat of bankruptcy entails both explicit and implicit costs, firms will limit their debt ratios in order to avoid it. For any given debt level, the threat of bankruptcy is greater as the degree of business risk increases. Thus we would expect an inverse relationship between corporate debt ratios and perceived business risk.

Unfortunately, perceived business risk is notoriously difficult to measure. A possible proxy for investors' risk perceptions in a given year is the standard deviation of monthly percentage stock price changes for that year. Estimates of these standard deviations, derived from Standard and Poor's Composite Index for the years 1900–1980, are shown in figure 1.4, plotted against the pattern of replacement value debt ratios.

Movements in stock price volatility are dominated by the tremendous fluctuations of the Depression era. Figure 1.4 thus offers some support for the argument made by many observers: Corporate debt ratios plunged in the wake of the huge increases in business risk during the Great Depression and then began a long and steady climb, as business risk consistently remained at lower levels in the postwar years.

However, the ability of this proxy for business risk to explain the shorter swings in corporate debt ratios is not very great. One might argue

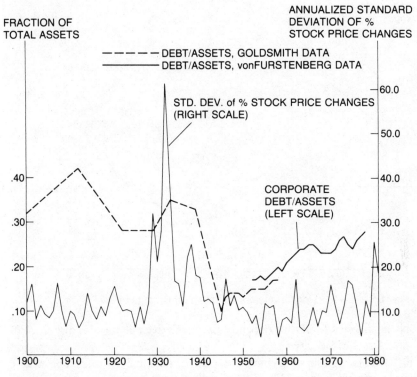

Fig. 1.4   Corporate debt ratios and perceived business risk

that the increased volatility around 1980 is associated with the reductions in debt financing that are apparent in the Federal Reserve Flow of Funds data in tables 1.2 and 1.3.[6] But the sharp changes in the debt ratio between 1900 and 1922 do not correspond to changes in volatility, and it is similarly difficult to match up most financing swings since 1960 with stock price fluctuations. Overall, the evidence that perceived business risk continually and consistently affects corporate financing patterns is limited.

1.2.2 Corporate and Personal Taxes

It is commonly held that the tax deductibility of interest favors debt over equity financing. From an investor's standpoint, however, interest is taxable at ordinary income rates, whereas a substantial fraction of the returns to equity are taxed at lower capital gains rates. The degree to which the tax advantage of debt at the corporate level outweighs its disadvantage

---

6. Other measures indicate an increase in business risk around this time as well. Wood (1981), for example, shows that the volatility of real interest rates increased sharply after 1972. Bodie et al. (1984) show that the real risk premium on long-term bonds suddenly jumped in 1979.

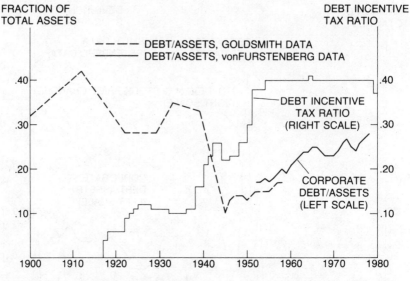

Fig. 1.5   Corporate debt ratios and income tax rates

at the investor level thus depends on the relative magnitudes of corporate and personal tax rates.

There is, of course, a whole spectrum of personal tax rates, and what is really needed is some idea of the distribution of investor wealth across tax brackets. In the absence of such information, a cruder measure, which I label the "debt incentive tax ratio," has been constructed as a proxy for the net tax advantage of corporate debt. It is essentially a comparison between statutory corporate tax rates and the lowest level of statutory personal rates.[7] This debt incentive tax ratio has been graphed in figure 1.5 against the replacement value debt ratio.

Figure 1.5 indicates that the biggest increase in the net tax advantage to corporate debt occurred between the late 1930s and early 1950s. The fact that this tax advantage has remained at a relatively high level for the past 40 years is undoubtedly related to the postwar increases in corporate debt. This tax advantage has been nearly constant for some time, though, so it cannot explain short-run fluctuations in the debt-equity mix. It is also something of a puzzle that debt financing proportions were high early in the century when there was no tax advantage and then fell after the tax code was introduced.

While there is little evidence of a close correspondence between movements in tax rates and corporate debt ratios, it is possible that some of the

7. Specifically, the debt incentive-tax ratio is $(tc - tp)/(1 - tp)$, where tc is the corporate tax rate and tp is the lowest personal rate. In Miller's (1977) model this measures the net tax advantage per dollar of corporate debt when investors have tax rate tp.

effect of tax considerations has been felt in more subtle ways. One could argue on the basis of table 1.4 that corporations have cut their dividend payouts somewhat in the wake of personal tax increases occurring in the 1940s and have thus substituted internal for external equity. In addition, tax considerations have clearly influenced the design of securities, apart from their relative proportions. This can be seen through such recent innovations as original-issue discount bonds, adjustable rate preferred stock, and the short-lived adjustable rate convertible note.

1.2.3 Inflation

Inflation is a third factor that is often thought to affect corporate financing proportions. One argument is that inflation enables corporations to repay their debt with cheaper dollars, but it is hard to understand why investors would not try to protect themselves through higher interest rates. A more sophisticated argument revolves around the fact that as it causes interest rates to rise, inflation increases the effective real tax deductions associated with debt. The inflation premium in interest rates is, of course, also taxable to investors, but as long as the corporate tax rate exceeds the personal rate of the marginal bondholder, inflation may cause the net tax advantage of corporate debt to increase.

In figure 1.6, annual inflation rates, as measured by percentage changes in the GNP deflator, are graphed against replacement value debt ratios. Although debt ratios have been relatively high in the inflationary years of the 1970s, it would be difficult to argue on the basis of figure 1.6 that there has been a close positive relationship between the movements in inflation rates and debt ratios.

Again, as with tax considerations, some of inflation's effects may manifest themselves in more subtle ways. To see one such effect, consider the role of corporations in the financial system: Corporations perform an intermediary role, purchasing and managing productive assets and, in effect, repackaging these assets for investors in the form of debt and equity claims. Purely financial intermediaries may perform further repackaging. Through term landing, for example, commercial banks transform long-term business debt into shorter- term deposits.

Now consider the effects of high and variable inflation rates on investors' demand for securities. If investors prefer short-term, or at least variable rate, securities in such an environment, and if commercial banks no longer find maturity intermediation a viable activity, nonfinancial corporations will have to perform this function themselves. That is, they will repackage more of their assets in the form of short-term and floating rate debt instruments. Thus inflation, and in particular uncertain inflation, may affect not so much the debt-equity mix, but rather the kinds of debt instruments corporations must issue to satisfy the needs of investors.

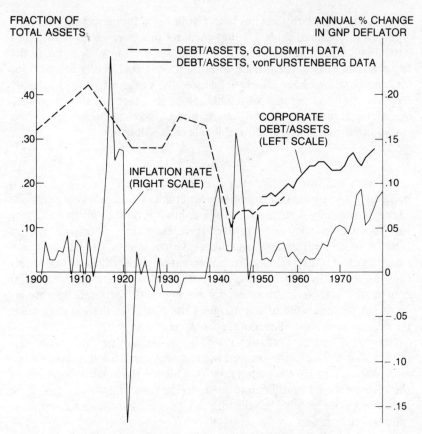

Fig. 1.6   Corporate debt ratios and inflation

1.2.4   Federal Government Borrowing

Corporate financing behavior should also be influenced by the behavior of other sectors in the financial system. For example, the supply of federal government debt will condition investors' willingness to absorb the relatively low-risk fixed claims represented by corporate debt. While not often cited as a determinant of the corporate financing mix, government borrowing may thus exert an important influence on the financing activities of the corporate sector as a whole.[8]

Evidence in support of such a relationship is presented in figure 1.7, in which the ratio of federal government debt to that of all domestic nonfinancial sectors is graphed against the replacement value debt ratio for corporations. There appears to be a strong inverse relationship between the

8. Exceptions include Friedman (1982) and Kaufman (1981).

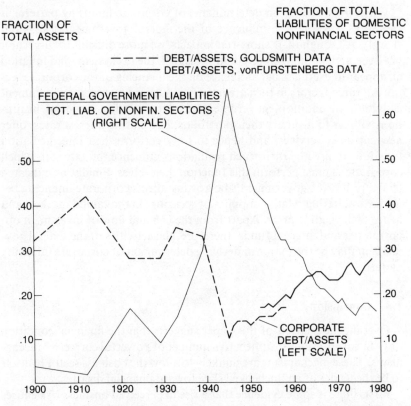

FRACTION OF
TOTAL ASSETS

FRACTION OF TOTAL
LIABILITIES OF DOMESTIC
NONFINANCIAL SECTORS

– – – – – DEBT/ASSETS, GOLDSMITH DATA
————— DEBT/ASSETS, vonFURSTENBERG DATA

FEDERAL GOVERNMENT LIABILITIES
TOT. LIAB. OF NONFIN. SECTORS
(RIGHT SCALE)

CORPORATE
DEBT/ASSETS
(LEFT SCALE)

Fig. 1.7   Corporate debt ratios and federal government borrowing

two series. In the early part of the century, when government debt was small, corporations satisfied investors' demands for safe, fixed claims by issuing large proportions of their own debt. Then, as federal borrowing swelled during the Depression years and World War II, corporate debt proportions fell drastically.

The inverse relationship is even more striking if we recall from table 1.4 that corporations held large proportions of government securities in 1945. Not only was the amount of government debt curtailing corporate debt proportions, but, in effect, corporations were repackaging some portion of that government debt in the form of corporate equity.

Following World War II, the trend in the share of government debt has been primarily downward, while corporate debt ratios have simultaneously drifted upward. Moreover, many of the short-term swings in government debt share have been mirrored by opposite movements in corporate debt proportions.

When the evidence on determinants of corporate financing patterns is viewed as a whole, the influence of the federal government stands out sharply. Although their short-run impacts are more difficult to discern, it has been argued that perceived business risk, the tax system, and inflation all appear to exert a broad influence on the financing of the corporate sector. All three factors in turn are heavily influenced by federal government activities. In addition, government regulations affect financial institutions' ability to diversify their portfolios, pay market interest rates, offer new customer services, and hence to fully perform their intermediation function. Indirectly, then, such regulations influence the extent to which corporations must perform this function themselves. Finally, as indicated by figure 1.7, the government's borrowing affects corporate financing behavior by altering relative supplies of securities in the capital markets and hence their relative price. Apart from the ebb and flow of investment opportunities and internal funds, therefore, the activities of the federal government may be the major underlying determinant of corporate financing patterns.

1.3 Conclusion

Overall, the analysis of this paper suggests that the financial condition of U.S. corporations is subject to a number of powerful corrective mechanisms. These mechanisms are unlikely to allow the business sector by itself to be the leader of an unchecked slide toward financial disaster.

First, there is some evidence that a rise in perceived business risk causes firms to moderate their reliance on debt financing. This tendency is hard to observe during short-run business cycle swings, but as business risk changes over prolonged periods it is more noticeable. It is certainly evident in the sharp cutback in debt proportions in the wake of the Great Depression, for example. It also seems likely that some of the moderation in debt financing in recent years has been motivated by perceptions of increased business risk.

Second, long-run balance sheet targets send strong danger signals when financing proportions get too far out of line. This is particularly apparent in the Flow of Funds data in tables 1.2 and 1.3, as debt financing was curtailed after reaching historically high levels during 1969–73.

Moreover, it does not appear that these traditional balance sheet targets have been adjusted for inflationary distortions. The data in table 1.3 suggest that, once corrections are made for changes in real indebtedness, corporate financial policies were quite conservative in recent years. This may stand as testimony to the difficulty of convincing lenders that traditional balance sheet ratios do not have the same meaning in inflationary periods. Indeed, U.S. corporations have severely curtailed dividend payments and have placed heavy reliance on internal funds since the mid-1970s in an effort to reduce their dependence on external suppliers of funds.

Finally, the behavior of other sectors in the capital market, particularly the federal government, can act as an important check on corporate borrowing. Any one corporation is probably small enough that it need not worry about the effect of its own securities issues on the relative supplies of different types of instruments. The corporate sector as a whole, by contrast, must compete with the other sectors who are primarily issuers of debt. As the federal government in particular increases its borrowing, investors' appetite for corporate debt will be less strong and corporations may turn toward other financing sources, especially internal equity.

While these forces act as checks against excessive risk taking, it should not be inferred that U.S. corporations face no financial problems whatsoever. In the presence of inflation and volatile interest rates, corporations have increasingly had to take on some of the intermediation functions that traditional financial institutions have no longer been able or willing to perform. This has led them to rely more heavily on short-term liabilities and has necessitated more frequent rolling over of their outstanding debt.

The outlook for inflation and economic stability, then, is one of the keys to future corporate financing patterns. These forces will determine whether corporations face the same sharp swings in internal funds availability that they experienced in the 1970s and early 1980s. They will also influence the allocation of financial intermediation activity between corporations and financial institutions.

A second major problem that business corporations face is the future course of government financing. To the extent that potential corporate borrowing is crowded out by the federal government, the corporate sector faces some potentially painful choices: it must cut dividends in order to increase internal funds, it must raise external equity, or it must cut back on capital spending.

In part, uncertainties about future corporate financing patterns reflect uncertainty over the future course of inflation, economic stability, and government borrowing. It should also be clear, however, that a good part of any residual uncertainty stems from the fact that we still have much to learn about these patterns. The effects of business risk, taxes, and inflation leave traces in the data, but these forces do not appear to be the whole story. Moreover, their effects are more subtle and more difficult to uncover than has commonly been thought.

At least two remaining issues require a better understanding. One of these is the behavior of equity issues. Why, for example, were corporations so much more willing to issue equity earlier in the century than they have been in the postwar years? Is this entirely a tax-related phenomenon, or are other forces at work? A second important issue is the precise nature of the linkage between the borrowing activity of the federal government and the financing, dividend, and investment policy of the corporate sector.

References

Bennett, A. 1984. Risky trend in business borrowing. *New York Times,* May 27.

Bodie, Z; Kane, A; and McDonald, R. 1984. Why haven't nominal rates declined? *Financial Analysts Journal* 40 (March/April): 16–27.

Business Week. 1974. The Debt Economy. Special Issue, October 12.

————. 1982. Debt's New Dangers. June 26.

Carson-Parker, J. 1981. The Capital Cloud over Smokestack America. *Fortune* February 23, pp. 70–80.

Friedman, B. M. 1982. Debt and economic activity in the United States. In *The Changing Roles of Debt and Equity in Financing United States Capital Formation,* edited by B. M. Friedman. Chicago: University of Chicago Press (for NBER).

Goldsmith, R. W. 1958. *Financial Intermediaries in the American Economy since 1900.* Princeton: Princeton University Press.

————. 1982. *The National Balance Sheet of the United States, 1953–1980.* Chicago: University of Chicago Press.

Goldsmith, R. W.; Lipsey, R. E.; and Mendelson, M. 1963. *Studies in the National Balance Sheet of the United States.* 2 vols. Princeton: Princeton University Press.

Gordon, R. H., and Malkiel, B. G. 1981. Corporation finance. In *How Taxes Affect Economic Behavior,* edited by H. J. Aaron and A. Pechman, Washington, D.C.: Brookings Institution.

Holland, D. M., and Myers, S. C. 1979. Trends in corporate profitability and capital costs. In *The Nation's Capital Needs: Three Studies,* edited by R. Lindsay. New York: Committee for Economic Development.

Kaufman, H. 1981. National policies and the deteriorating balance sheets of American corporations. Address to the Conference, February 25. New York: Salomon Brothers.

Mains, N. E. 1980. Recent corporate financing patterns. *Federal Reserve Bulletin* 66:683–90.

Massaro, G. 1977. *Corporate Capital Structures and Financing Patterns, 1977–80.* New York: Conference Board.

Miller, H. 1963. The corporation income tax and corporate financial policies. In *Stabilization Policies,* edited by Commission on Money and Credit. Englewood Cliffs, N.J.: Prentice-Hall.

————. 1977. Debt and taxes. *Journal of Finance* 32:261–75.

Mitchell, K. 1983. Trends in corporation finance. *Federal Reserve Bank of Kansas City Economic Review* 68 (March): 3–15.

Moran, M. J. 1984. Recent financing activity of nonfinancial corporations. *Federal Reserve Bulletin* 70:401–10.

Myers, S. C. 1984. The capital structure puzzle. *Journal of Finance* 39: pp. 575–92.

Shad, J. S. R. 1984. The leveraging of America. *Wall Street Journal.* June 28.

Taggart, R. A., Jr. 1985. Secular patterns in the financing of U.S. corporations. In *Corporate Capital Structures in the United States,* edited by B. M. Friedman, Chicago: University of Chicago Press (for NBER).

Von Furstenberg, G. M. 1977. Corporate investment: Does market valuation matter in the aggregate? *Brookings Papers on Economic Activity* 2:347–97.

Von Furstenberg, G. M., and Malkiel, B. G. 1977. Financial analysis in an inflationary environment. *Journal of Finance* 32:575–88.

Wood, J. H. 1981 Interest rates and inflation. *Economic Perspectives* (Federal Reserve Bank of Chicago) 5 (May/June): 3–12.

2   Debt and Equity Returns Revisited

Patric H. Hendershott

2.1 Introduction

In April 1981, near the beginning of the NBER project on corporate capital structures, I reported on the behavior of debt and equity returns over the last half-century. Resource utilization and inflation varied widely over that period, as did real and nominal ex post returns on debt and equity claims. My analysis of the factors affecting returns was based largely on a relatively crude examination of the data. I return three and a half years later (September 1984) with a shorter (quarter-century) perspective and with the benefit of extensive econometric testing.

Some of the findings discussed in this chapter are the same as those emphasized in my earlier paper. For example, a strong systematic relationship between ex post equity returns and business cycle turning points seemed to exist in my earlier analysis, with returns being extraordinarily large around cycle troughs and small around cycle peaks. This relationship is easily verifiable econometrically and is even stronger after 1980 than before. On the other hand, data from the 1951–80 period were largely consistent with Treasury bill rates moving one-for-one with expected inflation and being independent of everything else, a view obviously inconsistent with the high real short-term rates that have prevailed since 1980.

This chapter is divided into three broad parts and a short summary. I begin with an analysis of ex post returns on corporate bonds and equities, then turn to an examination of real after-tax 6-month bill rates, and conclude with an explanation of new issue coupons on 6-month and 20-year Treasury securities. Econometric results on the determinants of ex post re-

Patric H. Hendershott is professor of finance at Ohio State University, where he holds the John W. Galbreath Chair in Real Estate, and research associate of the National Bureau of Economic Research. The excellent research assistance of David Linn has been most beneficial.

turns and new issue coupons are summarized. The general procedure is to establish relationships on semiannual data from the 1950s, 1960s, and 1970s and then to deduce their applicability to the early 1980s.

2.2 The Business Cycle and Ex Post Equity and Bond Returns

My earlier study contained evidence that corporate equities systematically outperformed corporate bonds near business cycle troughs and underperformed them near business cycle peaks. The evidence was obtained by dividing the months between January 1926 and December 1978 into three types of periods: those around peaks, those around troughs, and the remainder. The peak periods were defined as the last 6 months of every expansion and the first half (dropping fractions) or first 6 months, whichever was less, of every contraction. The trough periods were defined as the last half (dropping fractions) or last 6 months, whichever was less, of every contraction and the first 6 months of every expansion. I then divided the total 1926–78 period into 10 overlapping intervals that contained single adjoining peaks and troughs and all the surrounding months that did not overlap with adjacent peak and trough periods. That is, the intervals extended from 6 months after a trough to 6 months before the second following peak.

These 10 overlapping intervals are listed at the left in table 2.1. Also reproduced are the arithmetic means (annualized) during the trough periods within the interval, the peak periods within the interval, the normal

Table 2.1   Annualized Difference between Returns on Equities and Bonds Near Troughs, Near Peaks, and in Other Periods (Percent)

	Near Troughs	Near Peaks	Other Months	Excess Near Troughs	Excess Near Peaks
Jan 26–Feb 29	35	20	21	14	−1
June 28–Nov 36	30	−4	1	29	−5
Oct 33–Aug 44	34	−32	8	26	−40
Jan 39–May 48	31	21	4	27	17
May 46–Jan 53	36	−9	13	23	−22
May 50–Feb 57	43	−5	21	22	−26
Dec 54–Oct 59	45	−11	18	27	−29
Nov 58–June 69	31	−12	8	23	−20
Sept 61–May 73	23	−13	5	18	−18
June 71–Dec 78	23	−9	−4	27	−5
Mean	33	−5	10	24	−15
Std. Dev.	7	16	9	5	17

Sources: Hendershott (1982, table 1.5, p. 25)

months (months not classified as either peak or trough months), and the differences in average returns between the peak and normal months and between the trough and normal months. The latter were labeled the excess net returns near peaks and troughs, respectively. As noted, the data were striking. The excess net returns on equities around troughs averaged 24%, and no net return was less than 14%. In contrast, the excess net returns on equities were negative around all peaks, except that at the end of World War II, and averaged −15%. When the analysis was restricted to the six cycles between 1946 and 1978, the average excess net return on equities around peaks was −20% and no return exceeded −5%.

These data raise three questions. First, are equity returns, bond returns, or both sensitive to the business cycle? Second, can a significant proportion of the variation in equity and/or bond returns during the 1953–79 period be explained by the business cycle turning points? Third, has the importance of the turning points continued in the 1980s? To answer these questions, I begin with a regression of ex post 6-month returns (times 2 to annualize them) on equities and bonds on constant terms and two turning-point variables. The variables assume values equal to the fraction of the half-year that consists of, respectively, peak or trough months as defined in the previous paragraph.[1] (Given that the average cycle is just under 5 years, the economy is near a peak about one-fifth of the time and near a trough another one-fifth.) The results are for the 54 semiannual observations in the 1953–79 period. As can be seen from the first equation summarized in table 2.2, all three variables are statistically significant in the equity equation (T-statistics are in parentheses under the coefficients), and 36% of the variation in 6-month returns is explained. Further, the second equation shows that while the trough variable is marginally significant in the bond returns equation, the peak variable adds no explanatory power and only 10% of the variation in bond returns is explained. Thus, the answers to the first and second questions are that the business cycle largely affects equity, not bond, returns and that the impact is large. In roughly the year surrounding business cycle troughs, the return on equities is 32 percentage points greater than the normal 9%. In roughly the year around peaks, the return is 20 percentage points less than the 9% norm.

This conclusion is supported by two additional tests reported in table 2.2.[2] In the first, I examine the excess of equity and bond returns over the 6-month bill rate at the beginning of the half-year. The results are changed little from the straight returns equations. Second, I add the unexpected

1. Cycle turning points through the January 1980 peak are listed in Hendershott (1982, table 1.3, p. 21). Since then the U.S. economy has experienced a trough in July 1980, a peak in July 1981, and a trough in November 1982.
2. See Hendershott and Huang (1985) for a wide variety of estimates.

Table 2.2   Response of Ex Post Corporate Equity and Bond Returns to the
                   Business Cycle, 1953–79

Dependent Variable (Annual Rate)	Constant Term	Response to			R^2	SEE	D-W
		Cycle Trough	Cycle Peak	Unanticipated Capital Gain			
Equity return	.090	.320	−.206		.36	.198	2.52
	(2.6)	(3.9)	(−2.6)				
Bond return	.027	.077	−.032		.10	.095	1.97
	(1.6)	(2.0)	(−0.9)				
Equity return less 6-month bill rate	.039	.339	−.214		.37	.202	2.43
	(1.1)	(4.1)	(−2.7)				
Bond return less 6-month bill rate	−.032	.114	−.039		.11	.135	1.99
	(1.4)	(2.3)	(−0.8)				
Bond return less 6-month bill rate	.004	−.003	−.022	1.107	.81	.045	2.03
	(0.4)	(−0.1)	(−1.2)	(13.3)			

Note: t-ratios are in parentheses beneath the estimated responses (coefficients).

capital gain on 20-year Treasury bonds during the 6-month period, UNCG, as a regressor, where

$$UNCG = \frac{UN\Delta R20}{R20} \frac{(1 + R20)^{20} - 1}{(1 + R20)^{20}}$$

and the calculation of unexpected change in the 20-year rate, $UN\Delta R20$, is described in Hendershott and Huang (1985, app. B). Forces causing unexpected capital gains (and thus large returns) on one asset will also induce large returns on assets that are close substitutes. The unexpected-gains variable has a negligible effect on equity returns but an enormous positive effect on corporate bond returns, as indicated by the last equation in table 2.2. Clearly corporate and Treasury bonds are very close substitutes, and thus unexpected Treasury rate changes explain most of the movement in ex post corporate bond returns. Also, the slight impact the trough cycle variable seems to have on corporate bond returns is due to a correlation between this variable and unexpected changes in the Treasury rate, not to the independent effect of the trough variable.[3]

3. While a number of proxies for unexpected capital gains on equities (or changes in its required rate of return) were tested in the equities equation, none significantly diluted the estimated impact of the turning-point variables.

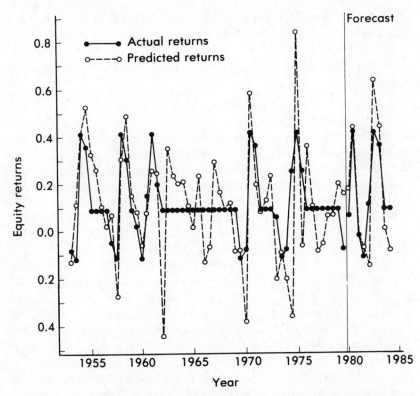

Fig. 2.1   Annualized 6-month equity returns, actual (A), predicted (P), and forecast, 1953–84

The actual and predicted (by the first equation in table 2.2) equity returns are plotted in figure 2.1. The 54 points to the left of the vertical line are in sample; the 9 points to the right are forecasts for the 1980–mid-1984 period. In sample the equation misses the entire early 1962 stock market plunge, much of the early 1970 (Cambodian incursion) crash, and more than the entire late 1974 decline. Of course, each of these market sell-offs, and the corresponding equation error, was largely reversed in the subsequent 6 months. (The general negative correlation of errors was indicated by the 2.52 Durbin-Watson ratio.)

The estimated equation is considerably more successful in explaining equity returns the 1980s than during the estimation period itself. Most of the large gains in 1980 and the mid-1982–mid-1983 period occurred in near-trough periods and thus are picked up by the equation. The root mean square error is 0.190, about the same as during the estimation period, but the volatility of returns so far in the 1980s has been far greater than in the previous quarter-century. The cycle dummies explain 72% of the variation of equity returns in the first half of the 1980s, about double the percentage explained during the estimation period.

As another measure of the forecasting ability of this equation, I computed the cumulative percentage forecast error over the nine semiannual periods as

$$CUMERR = \prod_{i=1}^{9} (1 + \frac{ERR_i}{2}) - 1,$$

where ERR_i is the error from the estimated equation in the ith period. The result is a negligible 0.003. That is, the 4½-year forecast of the stock market plus cumulative dividends is within a half percent of the actual. So our third question—Does the estimated cyclical influence on equities hold up in the 1980s?—is answered strongly in the affirmative.[4]

While the cycle dummy variables explain over a third of the variation in equity returns over the 1953–79 period, the variables obviously cannot explain extended market booms or busts, and there was, of course, a major market collapse between 1968 and 1978, with most of the decline coming after 1972. To illustrate the failure of our equation to capture this decline, unity plus the cumulative error over the 1953–79 period is plotted in figure 2.2. Along with it is Tobin's average q, the ratio of the market value (debt plus equity) of firms to the replacement cost of assets, as presented in the 1983 *Economic Report of the President* (table B-88, p. 263). The general correlation between the series, especially after 1962, is obvious. The existence of the 1969–78 decline and the failure of the regression equation to capture it explains the low (0.36) explanatory power in the 1953–79 period relative to the first half of the 1980s, when no prolonged decline (or increase) occurred.

Many explanations have been advanced for the 1969–78 stock market decline (see Hendershott [1981] for a summary and critique of most of them). That which I find most appealing, however, is the "relative factor price hypothesis," according to which unanticipated relative factor price changes caused previously optimal outstanding capital to become suboptimal. Given a putty-clay technology, the profitability of existing capital, and thus the value of ownership claims to this capital, declined in response to sharp revisions in expectations regarding factor prices. Most of the roughly one-third decline in q after 1972 can, in fact, be explained by unexpected factor price changes (Elmer and Hendershott 1984).

2.3 Nominal and Real Short-Term Interest Rates and Inflation

When I examined interest rates and inflation in early 1981, financial economists were still in the "Fama era" of constant real interest rates.

---

4. While hardly surprising, I note that ex post bond returns have continued in the 1980s to be largely explained by unanticipated changes in new issue coupon rates on 20-year Treasuries.

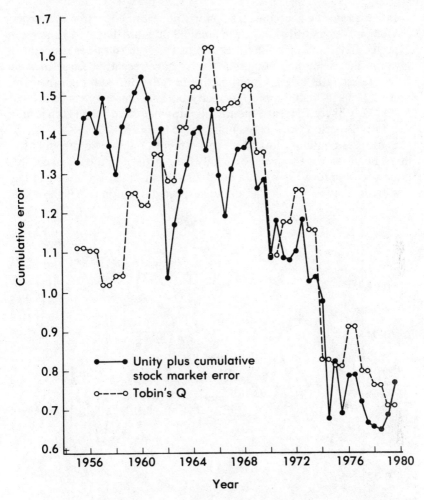

Fig. 2.2   Unity plus the cumulative stock market error since 1953 (E)
and Tobin's q (Q), 1955–79

Study after study of data from the 1950s, 1960s, and 1970s documented
the roughly one-for-one response of interest rates to changes in inflation.
Between 1952 and 1980, the real 1-month bill rate averaged 0.5% with a
standard deviation of only 1.5%. I noted, however, that the real bill rate
was not constant prior to 1951. Most important, the real rate exceeded 4%
in each year in the 1926–30 period.[5]

5. Between 1931 and 1951 the nominal bill rate was near zero, and thus the real rate was
roughly the negative of the inflation rate and ranged between 10% in 1931 and − 17% in
1946.

Interest rates have become a far more interesting topic in recent years. No longer is every little squiggle in nominal rates attributed to a change in expected inflation (although the St. Louis Fed seemed rather reluctant to give up this view), and numerous papers have recently been written on why interest rates are too high relative to inflation. And high they are. Since late 1980, real 6-month Treasury bill rates have averaged around 5.5%. Very likely, the real 6-month bill rate will exceed 4% in each year in the 1981–84 period, strikingly similar to the late 1920s.

Figure 2.3 contains plots of the real 6-month bill rate before and after tax. The bill rate is the average of daily figures (of beginning- and end-of-month data before 1960), on a bond-equivalent basis, for June and December of the years 1954–84, and the expected inflation rate is the corre-

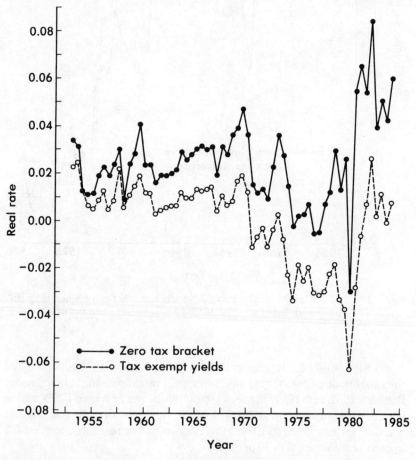

Fig. 2.3   After-tax 6-month bill rates for marginal investors in the zero tax bracket (Z) and in that bracket implied by tax-exempt yields (E), 1953–84

Table 2.3   **Real After-Tax Treasury Bill Rates**

	Nominal 6-Month Bill Rate	Expected 6-Month Inflation	Real After-Tax Rate Tax-Rate		Unanticipated Inflation
			0	0.423*	
1954–73	4.15	1.72	2.43	0.74	1.06
			(0.93)†	(0.78)†	
1974–mid-80	7.58	7.02	.85	−2.70	1.95
			(1.13)†	(0.66)†	
mid-80–mid-84	12.08	6.42	5.66	.25	−1.31
			(1.40)†	(1.58)†	

*This is unity less the average ratio of the yields on 12-year tax-exempt (prime grade) taxable (Treasury) securities over the 1954–84 period. The actual ratio for each period is employed in the calculations.

†The standard deviations of the real after-tax rates are reported in parentheses underneath the mean values.

Sources: The text and Hendershott (1984).

sponding number for 6-month inflation from the Livingston survey. The extraordinarily high level of real bill rates in the 1980s is obvious. In the eight observations from December 1980 to June 1984, the real bill rate averaged over 5.5%. This is 4 percentage points higher than the average of the 1960s and 1970s.

The appropriate tax rate to employ in a study of real after-tax bill rates is uncertain, and it would probably not be difficult to find economists who would advocate rates as low as zero and as high as the corporate tax rate. One possible way of determining the relevant tax rate is to compare the yields on high-quality tax-exempt securities with those on bills.[6] The real after-tax bill rate, according to this scheme, is then the tax-exempt rate less the expected inflation rate. This representation of the after-tax real bill rate, indicated by the dashed line in figure 3.3, tells a far different story than the before-tax real rate. In only one observation in the 1980s (June 1982) is the real after-tax rate out of line relative to the 1960s. The rate is high in the 1980s only relative to the extraordinarily low rates in the 1970s.[7]

The data in table 2.3 highlight the instability of real interest rates, whether the marginal tax rate of investors is as low as zero or as high as 0.4, during the last decade relative to the preceding two decades. The real

6. Unity less the ratio of prime grade 1-year municipal rates to 1-year Treasuries, both from Salomon Brothers and Hutzler, is utilized.

7. One extreme outlier in both rate series in recent years is worthy of note. The −3% real bill rate in June 1980 was 2.5% below any other observed bill rate in the entire period, and the −6.3% after-tax real rate was also 2.5% below any other. The record declines to unprecedented lows and the even sharper immediate reversals cry out for an extraordinary explanation. Fortunately, one is available. In March 1980, the Federal Reserve implemented a credit

rate based on a zero tax investor averaged 2.43% in the 1954–73 period with a standard deviation (listed in parentheses beneath the mean) of only 0.93%. For the remainder of the 1970s, the rate fell to 0.85%, and it then jumped to 5.66% during the last 4 years. In spite of the subdivision of the last decade into two parts, the standard deviation of the real rate within the last subperiod was 50% higher than during the entire earlier two decades. The increase in the standard deviation is an even greater 100% if the tax bracket implied by the ratio of exempt to taxable rates is utilized. Note that real after-tax rates based on this tax bracket are extraordinarily low in the 1974–mid-1980 period and are not higher in the 1980s than they were in the 1954–73 period.

The last column in table 2.3 contains the average difference between the rate of change in the consumer price index net of the shelter component (to exclude the impact of changes in home mortgage rates) for each 6-month period less that forecast by Livingston interviewees at the beginning of the period. Unanticipated inflation so measured averaged 1% in the 1954–73 period, 2% in the 1974–mid-1980 span (which included half of the first oil price shock and all of the second), and − 1.33% since then. For those who might think that actual inflation is a better measure of expected inflation than is the Livingston forecast, this unexpected inflation series should be subtracted from the real interest rates in table 2.3 to obtain preferred measures of real rates. This adjustment would increase the already enormous rise in real rates between the 1970s and 1980s by 3.25 percentage points.

Given that economists are unsure of even what the interest rate puzzle is—high real rates in the 1980s, low rates in most of the 1970s, or both—it should not be surprising that there is little agreement on the determinants of rates. Wilcox (1983) attributes the low real rates in the mid-1970s to supply shocks (to the increase in real import prices). Many, most notably Clarida and Friedman (1984), cite tight money for the higher rates in the 1980s until late 1982, and Hendershott and Shilling (1982) and deLeeuw and Holloway (1983) point to the business tax cuts and easy fiscal policy generally as the source of high rates. Others cite deregulation, volatile money growth, volatile interest rates, and so on.

2.4   An Explanation of Changes in New Issue Yields

Changes in new issue yields are of paramount importance to ex post bond returns. These changes are also important to ex post equity returns

---

controls program that included a non-interest-bearing reserve requirement of 15% on increses in credit. Apparently as a result, consumer installment credit outstanding contracted at an annual rate of 10.5% in the April-May period, the first decline since May 1975 and the largest reduction since World War II. The controls program was eased in late May and terminated on July 24, 1980.

insofar as real interest rates influence the business cycle. And while I would not overemphasize the importance of real rates—who would dare in light of the 1983–84 economic expansion?—there is no doubt that real rates matter. Thus I conclude this chapter with an examination of the determinants of changes in new issue rates.

Given the diverse views held by financial economists on the determinants of interest rates, a consensus interpretation of their views cannot be presented. I will simply summarize the findings of my research. My framework draws together two views of interest rate determination: the expectations theory, whereby expected changes in rates can be inferred from forward rates, and structural models of rates, in which unexpected changes in rates can be attributed to unanticipated changes in expected inflation, economic activity, monetary growth, and possibly other factors. The variables explained are the changes, over semiannual periods, in the 6-month and 20-year Treasury rates described earlier. For unanticipated changes in expected inflation and economic activity, I utilize the difference between actual data and Livingston Survey expectations of inflation 6 and 12 months in the future and of industrial production 6 months out; for monetary growth I use the difference between the current growth rate and that during the previous 2 years (no survey data are available). The data are described in Hendershott (1984). While the inflation expectations data are appropriate for the 6-month bill rate, they are obviously an extremely rough approximation to the expectations relevant to a long-term interest rate.

The results of this estimation are summarized in table 2.4, in which only coefficients on the key variables are reported. The bill rate equation is estimated on data beginning in 1960 when data for 12-month bills first became available; the estimation ends in 1979 in order to determine the ability of rate relations estimated prior to the 1980s to explain the movement of rates in the early 1980s. The equations explain about one-third of the changes in rates.

To no one's surprise, I trust, expected inflation matters. The 0.738 coefficient in the bill rate equation (with a standard error of 0.24) is consistent with the results of a large number of previous studies. The low (0.18) coefficient in the bond rate equation probably reflects a general tendency for long-run expected inflation to move by much smaller amounts than short-run expected inflation.

Possibly to the surprise of some, real activity also matters to debt yields.[8] These estimates suggest that, other things being equal, the 6-month bill rate will be about 2 percentage points higher when the economy is operating at 90% capacity than when it is at 70% capacity, and the 20-

---

8. Clarida and Friedman (1984) and Makin and Tanzi (1983) also report large real income effects.

Table 2.4   **Responses of the Treasury Bill and Bond Rates to Inflation and Industrial Production Surprises and to Expected Interest Rate Changes**

		Responses to		
Dependent Variable	Period of Estimation	Unexpected Change in Expected 6-Month Inflation	Unexpected Change in Industrial Production	Expected Change in the Rate
Change in 6-month bill rate	1960–79 (semiannual)	.738 (2.8)	.0746 (2.2)	.720 (1.9)
Change in 20-year Treasury bond rate	1953–79 (semiannual)	.180 (2.4)	.0307 (3.3)	.943 (1.6)

Note: The numbers in parentheses are t-ratios.
Sources: The first equation is described in Hendershott (1984). The second equation is entirely analogous, employing the same variables except for the 20-year Treasury bond rate and the expected change in it. These two variables are described in Hendershott and Huang (1984, app B).

year bond rate will be about three-quarters of a point higher. The cyclical movement of the real bill rate is obvious from figure 2.1, where high values occur around all business cycle peaks (1953, 1957, 1959, 1969, 1973, and 1979). Moreover, analysis, in a somewhat different framework, of the 1-month bill rate is fully consistent with this result. Hendershott and Huang (1984) conclude that the 1-month rate would be a full 2½ points higher.

Most surprising, at least to some academics, is the role of expected interest rate changes. Recent research has attacked the expectations theory of the term structure of interest rates; expected changes in rates implied by forward rates are said to have negative value in explaining ex post rate changes.[9] In contrast, the estimated coefficients reported in table 2.4 are close to the expected value of unity and are significantly positive at the 95% and 90% confidence levels, respectively.

The estimated (through December 1979) equations have been used to interpret the rise and fall in the rates between June 1978 and December 1982. Table 2.5 contains the results. Eighty percent (6.70 percentage points) of the 8.42 increase in the bill rate to December 1980 is explained

9. See Shiller et al. (1983) and Mankiw and Summers (1984). However, Fama (1983) finds a modest value in forecasts, and Brennan and Schwartz (1982) and Buser and Hendershott (1984) report evidence of short rates reverting toward long rates.

Table 2.5   The 1978–82 Interest Rate Cycle

	June 78 – Dec. 80/ June 81		Dec. 80/June 81 – Dec. 82	
	6-Month Bill	20-Year Bond	6-Month Bill	20-Year Bond
Change in Rate	8.42	4.80	−7.40	−2.26
Due to:				
Unexpected Change in Expected Inflation	5.16	1.14	−3.54	−.74
Unexpected Change in Industrial Production	.66	.39	−1.48	−.73
Change in Inflation Uncertainty	.53	.16	−.55	−.17
Other (largely expected change in the rate)	.35	−.42	−1.20	−.06
Total	6.70	1.27	−6.99	−1.70
Unexplained Change	1.72	3.53	−.41	−.56

December 1980 is considered the peak for the bill rate; June 1981 for the bond rate.

by the equation. Over 5 points is due to unexpected increases in anticipated inflation, two-thirds of a point to unexpected increases in output, one-half point to the increase in inflation uncertainty, and one-third point to other factors. Because the expected inflation rate rose by only 4.1 percentage points, the real interest rate increased by 4.3 percentage points. Of this rise, the estimated equation explains 2.6 (6.7 − 4.1) points, or 60%. The estimated relationship also explains 60% of the extraordinarily high average real bill rates in the early 1980s.

One and a half percentage points of the 2.6-percentage point explained increase in the real bill rate can be attributed to the unanticipated increases in industrial production, inflation uncertainty, and other factors noted above. However, the primary single factor contributing to the rise was unexpected increases in inflation far in excess of the actual 4.1-percentage-point increase. From mid-1978 to mid-1979, no increase was expected, but a 2-point rise occurred. From late 1979 to late 1980 half-point increases were anticipated, while the actual expected rate rose by another 2 points. In total, the cumulated unexpected increase in anticipated inflation over this span was a full 7 percentage points. Even though the estimated coefficient on expected inflation increases is only 0.74, implying that the nominal bill rate rises by only three-quarters of a point for every point of unanticipated increase in inflation, the forecasted nominal bill rate rises by 5.2 points because of this 7-point increase, and thus the real bill rate rises by over a full point.

Between the end of 1980 and the end of 1982, the bill rate declined by nearly 7.5 percentage points. Nearly 95% of this decline is explained by the estimation equation. All the factors that contributed to the early increase in the bill rate reversed themselves, inducing the decline. Unexpected declines in industrial protection, inflation uncertainty, and the catch-all "other" tended to lower the real rate by 3 percentage points, but a smaller decline in unexpected than in actual inflation, along with the only partial (0.74) response of nominal rates to unexpected changes in inflation, partially offset the decrease in the real rate.

This explanation of the bill rate cycle is remarkably good, in my less than humble opinion, because most of the unprecedented increase in rates and all of the decrease came after the estimation period. Two problems of the forecast should be noted, however. First, the equation does not pick up the interyear oscillations in either 1980 (due to the credit controls, see n. 7) or 1982. Second, the forecasted 6-month rate is 1⅓ percentage points above the actual value at the end of 1982 (the 1.72-point underestimate of the increase less the 0.41-point underestimate of the decrease). That is, the real rate is 1⅓ points too high (relative to 1978), possibly due to some of the factors discussed earlier but not captured in our equation.

A similar, but far less satisfactory, explanation of the bond rate cycle is also summarized in table 2.5. The inability to explain much more than a quarter of the rise in this rate almost certainly follows from the inadequacy of the 6-month expected inflation rate as a proxy for long-run expected inflation. Long-run expected inflation likely rose by about as much as short-run expected inflation did in the 1978–80 period, but the 0.18 coefficient on the unexpected change in expected inflation translates the increase in expected inflation into an impact on the bond rate that is only one-quarter as large as that on the bill rate. The ability of the equation to explain three-quarters of the decline in the bond rate suggests that long-run expected inflation has not fallen nearly as much as short-run expected inflation, which seems quite plausible in light of the large outyear structural deficits.

2.5 Summary

A strong relationship has existed between ex post equity returns and business cycle turning points since at least 1926. Somewhere around business cycle peaks—during the last half-year of the expansion or the first half of the contraction—investors sharply reduce their expectations regarding future returns on equities, and the reverse occurs around business cycle troughs—during the last half of recessions and the first 6 months of upswings. As a result, stock prices rise near troughs and fall near peaks. During the 1953–79 period, ex post equity returns were 32% greater than the 9% norm in the year (roughly) surrounding troughs, and 21% less than the norm in the year surrounding peaks. This cyclical phenomenon alone explains over a third of the movement in returns. In the first nine semiannual periods in the 1980s, forecasts of returns based on the 1953–79 relationship explain over 70% of the movement in returns, and the cumulative error of a forecast of the stock market and cumulative dividends is less than 1%. Stock market performance so far in the 1980s has not been at all unusual.

In contrast, the level of real interest rates so far in the 1980s differs markedly from the prior quarter (nearly half) century. Nominal Treasury bill rates moved one-for-one, or slightly less, with changes in expected inflation during the 1951–79 period, resulting in relatively constant real bill rates which averaged 2%. In the 1980s, real rates have averaged over 5½%, duplicating the experience of the late 1920s. The source of the present high real rates is unclear, with various authors citing tight money (at least until late 1982), increased volatility of interest rates and monetary growth, easy fiscal policy, business tax incentives, and deregulation, among other reasons. More important, on an after-tax basis real rates are no higher now than in the 1950s and 1960s. What was unusual were the low real after-tax rates in the 1970s.

My own research on new issue Treasury coupon rates draws on two views of interest rate determination: the expectations theory, whereby expected changes in rates can be inferred from forward rates, and structural models of rates in which unexpected changes in rates can be attributed to unanticipated changes in expected inflation, economic activity, monetary growth, and possibly other factors. The first important result is the consistency of the data with the expectations theory. While expected rate changes explain little of observed changes in new issue rates, the data are consistent with the expectations theory. A second result is a strong positive relationship between Treasury rates and economic activity. As operation of the economy increases from 70% of capacity to 90%, real Treasury rates rise by 2½ percentage points at the short (1-month) end of the term structure to three-quarters of a point at the long (20-year) end.

In spite of the "success" of this research, the difficulties of forecasting interest rates should be obvious. Expected changes in rates explain a minuscule of 2% of actual changes because surprises are so prevalent. Moreover, "knowing" inflation, real activity, and money surprises increases the ex post explanatory power only to one-third. My sympathy goes to those forecasting interest rates for a living.

References

Brennan, M. J., and Schwartz, E. S. 1982. Bond pricing and market efficiency. *Financial Analysts Journal* 49–56.

Buser, S. A. and Hendershott, P. H. 1984. Pricing default-free fixed-rate mortgages. *Housing Finance Review* 3 (October):405–30.

Clarida, R. H., and Friedman, B. M. 1984. The behavior of U.S. short-term interest rates since October 1979. *Journal of Finance* 39 (July), 671–82.

DeLeeuw, F., and Holloway, T. M. 1983. The measurement and significance of the cyclically adjusted federal budget. Mimeographed, December.

Elmer, P. J., and Hendershott, P. H. 1984. Relative factor prices changes and equity prices. NBER Working Paper 1449, September.

Fama, E. 1983. The information in the term structure. Working Paper. no. 111, Center for Research in Security Prices, University of Chicago, October.

Hendershott, P. H. 1981. The decline in aggregate share values: taxation, valuation errors, risk and profitability. *American Economic Review* 71 (December), 909–22.

————. 1984. Expectations, surprises and Treasury bill rates: 1960–82. *Journal of Finance* 39 (July), 685–96.

————. 1982. Inflation, resource utilization, and debt and equity returns. *In The Changing Roles of Debt and Equity in Financing United States Capital Formation,* edited by B. M. Friedman. Chicago: University of Chicago Press (for NBER).

Hendershott, P. H., and Huang, R. D. 1985. Debt and equity yields: 1926–80. In *Corporate Capital Structures in the United States,* edited by B. M. Friedman. Chicago: University of Chicago Press (for NBER).

Hendershott, P. H., and Shilling, J. D. 1982. Capital allocation and the Economic Recovery Tax Act of 1981. *Public Finance Quarterly* 2:242–73.

Makin, J. H., and Tanzi, V. 1983. The level and volatility of interest rates in the United States: the role of expected inflation, real rates, and taxes. NBER Working Paper 1167, July.

Mankiw, N. G., and Summers, L. H. 1984. Do long-term interest rates overreact to short-term interest rates? *Brookings Papers on Economic Activity* 1:223–42.

Shiller, R. J.; Campbell, J. Y.; and Schoenholtz, K. L. 1983. Forward rates and future policy: interpreting the term structure of interest rates. *Brookings Papers on Economic Activity* 1:173–217.

Wilcox, J. A. 1983. Why real interest rates were so low in the 1970's. *American Economic Review* 73:44–53.

3 Risk and Required Returns on Debt and Equity

Zvi Bodie, Alex Kane, and Robert McDonald

One of the most striking developments in the United States capital markets during the past decade has been an enormous increase in the riskiness of long-term bonds and other fixed income securities. This has stemmed in part from increased inflation uncertainty and in part from fundamental shifts in Federal Reserve policies. In this paper we measure this phenomenon and explore its implications for the returns required by investors on these debt instruments and the equity securities which can substitute for them in wealth portfolios. We believe that our results help to explain why real interest rates on long-term bonds have been so high in recent years.

The data set used in the paper also enables us to address a different, although somewhat related, issue in the study of United States financial markets: Why, despite the apparent increase in inflation risk in the recent past, has no private market for indexed bonds developed in the United States?

The paper is organized as follows. We first discuss alternative approaches to estimating risk premiums on debt and equity securities and then explain our approach, which is based on modern portfolio theory. We apply our model to data on common stocks and on United States government bonds of eight different maturities to estimate risk premiums for the period 1973–83. Next we estimate the risk premium on Treasury bills relative to a hypothetical riskless real rate of interest over that same period. Finally, we discuss the implications of our model for the question why no private market for index-linked bonds exists in the United States.

Zvi Bodie is professor of finance and economics, Boston University School of Management, and is a research associate at the National Bureau of Economic Research. Alex Kane is associate professor of finance, Boston University School of Management, and is a research fellow at the National Bureau of Economic Research. Robert McDonald is assistant professor of finance, Northwestern University Graduate School of Management, and is a research fellow at the National Bureau of Economic Research.

3.1 Estimating Risk Premiums

All investors, be they individual or institutional investors seeking to allocate funds or a nonfinancial business entity seeking to acquire funds, are faced with choosing the proportions of debt and equity in their portfolio. Making this decision requires knowing both the expected rates of return on assets and the riskiness of those assets. A basic tenet of financial economies is that in equilibrium, expected returns on the various traded assets will reflect the perceived risk inherent in them. In a capital market dominated by risk-averse investors, the riskier the asset the higher the premium it will have to bear over the riskless rate of interest. This premium is usually called the "risk premium," and in general it is unobservable.

In order to make their investment and financing decisions, all parties involved must quantify their beliefs regarding the relative magnitudes of these risk premiums. Traditionally there have been two generic approaches to estimating risk premiums: (1) statistical estimation based on ex post data and (2) estimation based on economic models of security price formation coupled with forecasts of the fundamental variables in the models (e.g., earnings forecasts for stocks, the yield curve for bonds). Most analysts have used some combination of these two approaches.

Often one or even both of these approaches results in estimated risk premiums for some assets which violate one's criterion of "reasonableness," based on the perceived risk of those assets. For example, in many studies, past rates of return are used to compute means, variances, and covariances. The means are then taken as measures of expected future returns and the variances and covariances as measures of risk. Unfortunately, at times some of the risk premiums implied by the estimated means bear a relationship to the estimated risk measures, which contradicts the theory underlying the study.

Our approach is to use past data solely to obtain risk measures and then to compute the corresponding risk premiums implied by theory. Our reason for ignoring the estimated means is that, in order to get a reliable estimate of the mean of a stochastic time series, it is necessary to observe it over a long span of time. If the mean is changing over the period of observation, reliable estimation is virtually impossible. Variances and covariances, however, can be measured fairly accurately over much shorter sample periods.[1]

We view our approach as a supplement to other, more traditional methods of estimating risk premiums and think that it can be used to check the reasonableness of the estimates which they provide.

---

1. See Merton (1980) for a full discussion of this point.

3.2 The Model

The theoretical model we employ is a modified version of the capital asset pricing model, which has become the standard financial model of capital market equilibrium over the past two decades and has gained widespread acceptance within the financial industry under the name Modern Portfolio Theory (MPT). The fundamental insight of this model is that the riskiness of an individual asset is not its volatility or riskiness considered in isolation but rather its contribution to the risk of a portfolio of assets. The model has most frequently been used in the past to explain the structure of required returns on common stocks, but it applies just as well to all other traded assets, including bonds.

This theory implies that in equilibrium, the risk premium on any traded asset can be expressed as the product of two terms:

(1)   risk premium on asset i =
average degree of risk aversion of market participants $\times$
covariance of asset i with the market portfolio.

The first term, the average degree of risk aversion,[2] is the same for all assets, and thus at any point in time is simply a constant of proportionality. The second term, the covariance with the market portfolio,[3] is thus the critical determinant of differences in risk premiums across asset categories.

The market portfolio is by definition composed of all existing assets in the economy, each held in proportion to its relative outstanding supply. The covariance of any asset with the market portfolio is the sum of two factors: (1) the relative supply of that security times its own variance and (2) a weighted sum of its covariances with all other assets.

To facilitate our understanding of the empirical results to follow, let us examine how these factors work for the case of three categories of assets: stocks, bonds, and bills. Let us assume that the market portfolio consists of 65% stocks, 10% bonds, and 25% bills and that bills are riskless. The risk premiums would then be

risk premium on stocks = risk aversion $\times$ (.65 variance of stocks +
.1 covariance between stocks and bonds)

risk premium on bonds = risk aversion $\times$ (.1 variance of bonds +
.65 covariance between stocks and bonds).

---

2. The measure of risk aversion referred to is Pratt's coefficient of relative risk aversion. The higher the value of this coefficient, the greater the compensation an investor requires to bear a given degree of risk. For a complete explanation see Bodie et al. (1985).

3. The covariance referred to here is the covariance between the real rate of return on security i and the real rate of return on the market portfolio.

In the results presented in the next section we will refer to the correlation coefficient between asset returns rather than the covariance. The correlation coefficient is a more familiar measure of comovement in returns, and it is related to covariance by the following formula:

covariance between stocks and bonds = correlation coefficient × standard deviation of stocks × standard deviation of bonds.

The standard deviation is the square root of variance.

In the following section we estimate what the risk premiums implied by this model were over the period 1973–83 on 10 categories of financial assets: common stocks, bills, and United States government bonds of eight different maturity classes. Our measure of a bond's life is duration rather than the conventional measure of maturity. Duration is a weighted average of the times until each payment (coupon and principal) made by the bond, and may be used to compare consistently bonds with very different payment streams, for which maturity may provide a misleading comparison. A bond's price volatility is also more directly related to duration than to maturity.[4]

We follow the usual practice of computing the risk premiums on stocks and bonds relative to the rate of return on bills. Since bills are not completely riskless in real terms, this requires a slight modification in equation (1). The modification is as follows:

(1′)   risk premium on asset i relative to bills =
risk aversion × (covariance of asset i with the market portfolio − covariance of bills with the market portfolio).

3.3   Implied Risk Premiums on Stocks and Bonds

Consider a representative investor who goes to the market on the first day of each month and adjusts his portfolio according to his current views on the risk-return profile of different types of investments. We assume that the investor has the choice of the 10 different categories of financial assets mentioned at the end of the previous section, stocks, bills, and bonds of eight different durations.

---

4. Duration is defined by Macaulay (1938). The distinction between maturity and duration is important, because the duration of bonds of a given maturity shortened considerably in the late 1970s. For coupon bonds and mortgages, duration is always less than maturity. The difference between maturity and duration for ordinary coupon bonds and mortgages is greater, the longer the final maturity and the higher the level of interest rates. In 1953, the average maturity of the bonds in our 8-year duration portfolio was just under 9 years; in 1981, the average maturity was 23 years. This variation calls into question the appropriateness of a bond-return series with a constant maturity of 20 years, such as the one tabulated by Ibbotson and Sinquefield (1982).

The 10 different types of assets have been ordered according to their usual degree of riskiness, with 1-month Treasury bills carrying the least risk and (a diversified portfolio of common) stocks the most. In this context, "risky" refers to unexpected changes in security prices during the 1-month holding period. Changes in the yield curve will lead to capital gains or losses on fixed interest debt, and owners of common stocks will also be unable to predict with great accuracy the value of their holdings 1 month in the future.

In our estimation using United States data we assume that investors look back on the most recent 24 months when they estimate the volatilities of the different returns. We hold constant the degree of risk aversion[5] at 3.5 and the relative weights of the different categories in the market portfolio at roughly 65% stocks, 10% bonds, and 25% bills.[6] All change in the risk premiums over time is therefore coming from changes in the variances and correlations among asset categories.

An Appendix details our data sources and the precise procedure used for generating our time series, but it is possible to explain the general procedure in a fairly straightforward manner: Each month we use the model to forecast expected returns for the next month. Actual returns on stocks and bonds in any period will deviate from these forecasts. Investors will observe these forecast errors and use this information to improve upon their estimates of the variances and correlations attached to the 10 categories of risky investments. They do this by using data for the most recent 24 months. As we proceed through time, the estimates change and so too do the risk premiums required in order to compensate for the perceived risk.

Figure 3.1 illustrates the results of this procedure in computing the standard deviations for stock and long-term bond returns. It shows the standard deviation of the forecast errors in the monthly rate of return on our diversified portfolio of common stocks and in the monthly rate of return on long-term government bonds. Assuming no change in correlations, the pattern of risk premiums should follow the pattern of standard deviations. Figure 3.2 shows the corresponding risk premiums on stocks and on long-term bonds. We emphasize that these risk premia are computed relative to the return on T-bills.

The most striking aspect of these figures is the dramatic increase in the volatility of long-term bonds starting in the last quarter of 1979, coinciding with a basic change in Federal Reserve operating procedure. Between

---

5. For a discussion of why 3.5 is a reasonable number to use for the degree of risk aversion, see Bodie et al. (1985).

6. The relative weights of assets in the market portfolio changed over the period 1973–83, but it is shown in table AIV of Bodie et al. (1984) that the changes had only a small effect on risk premiums.

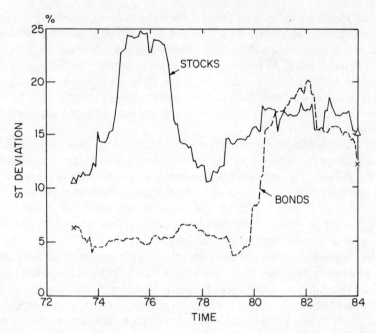

Fig. 3.1   Standard deviation of real rates of return on stocks and bonds, 1973–84

October 1979 and August 1982 the Fed was targeting monetary aggregates rather than interest rates, and as a result created a considerable increase in bond price volatility.

The volatility of stock prices peaked at about 22% in the period from 1975 to 1977. It subsequently declined, and has fluctuated in a range from 12% to 17% since 1979. In the period 1981–83 the volatility of long-term bond prices actually exceeded that of stocks, although by the end of the period they were about equal.

The risk premiums on stocks and bonds in figure 3.2 closely follow the time profiles of standard deviations shown in figure 3.1. But despite the rough equality in their standard deviations during 1982–83, the risk premium on stocks is roughly double that on long-term bonds. This is primarily because stocks constitute a much larger proportion of the market portfolio than do long-term bonds.[7]

7. To be more precise, the covariance of stocks with the market portfolio is approximately .65 × variance of stocks + .1 × covariance between stocks and bonds, while the covariance of bonds with the market portfolio is approximately .1 × variance of bonds + .65 × covariance between stocks and bonds. The covariance between stocks and bonds is much smaller than the variance of stocks or bonds. Even though the variance of bonds and stocks were roughly equal in 1982–83, the covariance of stocks with the market (and therefore the risk premium on stocks) was greater because the variance term has a weight of .65 for stocks vs. .1 for bonds.

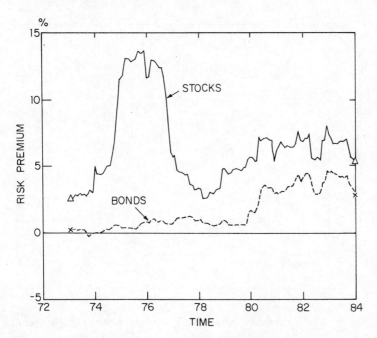

Fig. 3.2   Risk premiums on stocks and bonds, 1973–84

Note that while the volatility of long-term bonds has been falling more or less steadily since the end of 1981, the risk premium has not. After falling precipitously at the end of 1981 and the beginning of 1982, it climbed back to its previous high before starting to come down again in 1983. In order to understand this seemingly odd behavior of the risk premium on bonds we must look at the correlation between bond and stock returns.

Figure 3.3 shows the behavior of the correlation coefficient between bonds and stocks. It rose steeply between the beginning of 1981 and the end of 1982, which served to counteract the effect of a declining bond price volatility on the risk premium on bonds.[8]

Table 3.1 shows the risk premiums on all asset categories other than bills at three different points in time. Focusing on the December 1983 column, we see that the risk premiums on bonds rise more or less uniformly with maturity class. Starting with .53% for the shortest, it rises to 3% for duration 6 and then levels off. It should be emphasized that these risk pre-

---

8. We can express the covariance of bonds with the market portfolio approximately as

.1 × variance of bonds + .65 × (correlation between stocks and bonds × standard deviation of stocks × standard deviation of bonds)

A rise in the correlation between stocks and bonds can offset a decline in the variance of bonds and keep the covariance of bonds with the market (and therefore the risk premium on bonds) from falling.

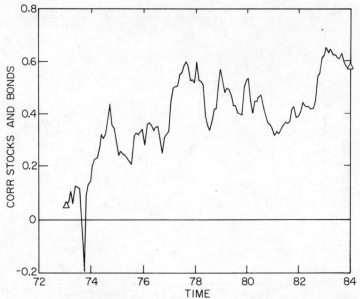

Fig. 3.3   Correlation between the real rates of return on stocks and bonds, 1973–84

Table 3.1   **Estimated Annual Risk Premiums (percent per year)**

	September 1979	December 1981	December 1983
Bonds:	.17	.77	.53
1	.27	1.47	.97
2	.42	1.67	1.18
3	.43	2.17	1.82
4	.52	2.48	2.15
5	.45	2.40	3.02
6	.41	3.48	2.89
7	.53	4.20	2.85
8			
Stocks	4.93	6.96	5.51

Note: Risk premiums calculated relative to rate of return on Treasury bills. Market weights are those for 1980, with pension fund reserves weighted for long durations.

miums are annualized rates of return in excess of the 1-month bill rate, which are expected to prevail over the next 1-month holding period. They are not yields to maturity. The risk premium on stocks is about 5.5%.

Going across the columns in table 3.1 we see that the risk premium on stocks rose from about 5% in 1979 to 7% in 1981 and then back down to

5.5% in 1983. That same general pattern is evident for all of the bonds too. Duration 8 bonds, for example, rose from about .5% in 1979 to 4% in 1981 and then back down to 3% in 1983. Bonds have clearly not returned as closely to their 1979 levels as have stocks.

Table 3.2 shows the standard deviations and correlation matrices underlying the risk premiums in table 3.1. Note that, as suggested by the behavior of risk premiums in table 3.1, the increase in standard deviation after October 1979 was greater for longer-duration bonds.

Table 3.2   Standard Deviations and Correlations of Real Rates of Return

	Common stocks	One-Month Bills	Bonds (duration in years)							
			1	2	3	4	5	6	7	8
			October 1977 – September 1979							
Standard deviation (% per year)	17.46	1.24	2.26	3.43	4.04	5.25	5.02	4.64	5.38	5.43
Correlation coefficients:										
Stocks		.37	.33	.37	.31	.31	.07	.21	.23	.25
Bills			.69	.64	.56	.58	.37	.31	.40	.36
Bonds: 1				.78	.79	.76	.76	.74	.79	.69
2					.90	.88	.76	.69	.74	.74
3						0.93	.87	.76	.82	.85
4							.84	.74	.78	.80
5								.85	.86	.89
6									.90	.80
7										.86
			January 1980 – December 1981							
Standard deviation	17.55	1.00	5.15	9.60	12.5	14.4	16.9	18.5	19.4	20.4
Correlation coefficients:										
Stocks		.13	.29	.29	.23	.28	.27	.24	.36	.41
Bills			.56	.49	.51	.47	.44	.36	.48	.43
Bonds: 1				.95	.91	.88	.85	.74	.82	.86
2					.95	.94	.90	.83	.88	.90
3						.98	.95	.86	.90	.91
4							.96	.86	.92	.93
5								.89	.93	.90
6									.92	.88
7										.93

Table 3.2 (*continued*)

	Common stocks	One-Month Bills	Bonds (duration in years)							
			1	2	3	4	5	6	7	8
			January 1982 – December 1983							
Standard deviation	15.04	1.08	3.00	4.59	5.85	7.84	9.31	10.63	11.81	11.91
Correlation coefficients:										
Stocks		.17	.45	.50	.48	.54	.54	.67	.55	.57
Bills			.53	.42	.31	.34	.28	.26	.26	.15
Bonds: 1				.95	.91	.88	.87	.82	.80	.73
2					.97	.90	.94	.89	.88	.83
3						.90	.97	.90	.91	.88
4							.92	.91	.90	.90
5								.95	.96	.93
6									.92	.94
7										.96

3.4   The Riskless Real Rate of Interest and the Risk Premium on Treasury Bills

Up to this point we have followed the conventional practice of measuring risk premiums relative to Treasury bills. While 1-month T-bills offer a risk-free nominal rate of return, uncertainty about the rate of inflation over the next month makes their real return risky. This inflation risk, however, is small relative to the risk of unanticipated stock and bond price changes during the month. Furthermore, for holding periods longer than 1 month, a policy of rolling over 30 day T-bills has been shown to offer a relatively stable real rate of return, because nominal bill rates can adjust rapidly to the changing inflation rate.

Nonetheless it is instructive to see what our model implies about the risk premium on T-bills over the 1973–83 period, particularly in the light of the increase in real bill rates in the 1980s. Perhaps we can explain at least part of this increase on the basis of increased covariance with the market portfolio, the way we did with bonds.

Figure 3.4 shows the behavior of the risk premium implied by equation (1), which says that it should be proportional to the covariance of the real rate of return on bills with the market portfolio. It should be remembered that the risk premium for bills is relative to a hypothetical risk-free real rate of interest. It is clear from figure 3.4 that, if anything, the risk premium on T-bills has declined rather than risen in the 1980s. If we want to understand why real bill rates have risen we must seek other explanations.

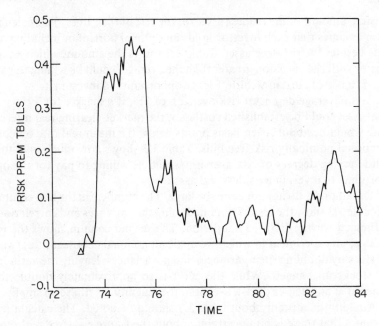

Fig. 3.4   Risk premium on 1-month Treasury bills, 1973–84

3.5 A Private Market for Indexed Bonds

A recurrent theme in both the popular and technical finance literature has been the issue of indexed bonds, that is, bonds whose principal and interest payments are linked to some index of the cost of living and are therefore riskless in real terms. Economists from different sides of the ideological spectrum, like Milton Friedman and James Tobin, find themselves in agreement on the desirability of having the federal government issue such an asset.

Some critics of this idea have argued that if index-linked bonds were a worthwhile innovation, the private capital markets would already have produced them. The data and theoretical model which we employed earlier in this paper can be extended to shed some additional light on this matter.[9]

We computed the value to investors of a private market for indexed bonds in the following way: first, we found the real risk-free rate at which an investor whose degree of risk aversion is equal to the average would be indifferent to holding this riskless asset. (If the asset is privately supplied, it will necessarily be priced so that the average investor is indifferent about holding it.) Then, we asked what one-time dollar payment each investor would be willing to make in order for them to obtain the right to hold the

9. Details behind the calculations in this section are contained in Bodie et al. (1985).

desired amount of the riskless asset for the rest of their lives. This calculation assumes that each investor holds an optimal portfolio, including assets besides the risk-free asset. Table 3.3 shows the amount which an investor with risk aversion greater than the average would be willing to pay, per $10,000 of current wealth, for the opportunity to invest in it.

At an average degree of risk aversion of 3.5, if a market for a riskless real asset could be established costlessly, the market-clearing real interest rate would be about seven basis points below the mean real rate on conventional nominally risk-free bills. Table 3.3 shows how much investors with varying degrees of risk aversion would be willing to pay for the opportunity to invest in a riskless real asset.

The amounts do not appear to be large. The numbers in the first column of table 3.3 show the results obtained using the variances and correlations estimated for the 1982–83 subperiod. The second column shows the results of an experiment in which we made all nominal debt securities twice as risky by doubling their variances and covariances, leaving the variance of stocks unchanged. While the effect is to approximately double the amount at any degree of risk aversion, the magnitudes still seem small.

An additional point about table 3.3 should be noted. The calculation assumes that there is no uncertainty about the future risk-free real rate. Thus, there is no distinction between indexed bills and indexed bonds. The numbers in table 3.3 apply equally to both assets.

Our explanation for these results is that conventional 1-month bills are a fairly good low-risk alternative to stocks and bonds even for very risk-averse investors. The extra safety of real return provided by an indexed bond is not worth much to them.

These results suggest one possible reason for the nonexistence of index bonds in the United States capital market. Since there would probably be some costs associated with creating a new market for such securities, the benefits would have to exceed those costs. Given the assumptions of our model, in particular the assumption that all market participants have the

Table 3.3   Willingness to Pay for the Opportunity to Invest in a Real Riskless Asset (Dollars per $10,000 of Wealth)

	Willingness to Pay	
Coefficient of Relative Risk Aversion	Actual Variances and Covariances (1982–83)	Double All Variances And Covariances But Stocks
3.5	0	0
5	$6.50	$13
6	16	32

same set of price expectations, the benefit from trading in these new securities would have to arise from differences in the degree of risk aversion among investors. If, as table 3.3 suggests, the willingness to pay does not appear to be large over a fairly broad range of risk aversion coefficients, then one should not be surprised at the failure of a private market for index bonds to appear.

3.6 Summary and Conclusions

It appears that there may have been a substantial rise in risk premiums on long-term bonds in the early 1980s as a market response to an increase in bond price volatility and an increased correlation between bond and stock returns. The increase in bond price volatility was sudden and coincided with a shift in Federal Reserve policy to stabilizing monetary aggregates rather than interest rates starting in the last quarter of 1979. Despite a fall in the long-term expected rate of inflation, long-term interest rates may have remained high during this period, at least partially because of this risk premium.

By the end of 1983 the risk premium on bonds had fallen considerably from its peak and was trending downward, reflecting a major decline in bond price volatility. These results suggest that Federal Reserve policy can have a profound effect on the level of long-term interest rates through the effect it has on their variability.

Appendix

We assume that there are 10 classes of assets—stocks, Treasury bills, and nominally risk-free (i.e., government) bonds of duration 1–8 years. We used monthly real rates of return taken from Ibbotson and Sinquefield's Treasury bill series, bond data from the United States government bond file of the Center for Research in Security Prices (CRSP), and stock returns from the New York Stock Exchange monthly CRSP file, adjusting when necessary by the consumer price index excluding the cost of shelter.

Land, residential housing, and consumer durables account for about 40% of household net worth. Unfortunately, there are no reliable rate of return data for a variety of assets that are not literally either stocks or bonds but that are often perceived as substitutes for those assets. Time and demand deposits, for example, are assumed to have the same rate of return as Treasury bills; corporate bonds and municipal bonds are assumed to be like government bonds; and noncorporate equity is assumed to have the same characteristics as equity. In preference to excluding these assets entirely from the market portfolio, we accept these assumptions and include these assets in the appropriate categories for the purpose of determining market weights.

In order to compute the covariance of the return on the market with the return on each asset category, we of course need to know the composition of the market portfolio (the market weights). Theoretically, this should reflect the percentage of household net worth invested in the assets that comprise the market portfolio. We used the *Flow of Funds Sector Balance Sheets* to obtain this breakdown for broad categories of assets for 1976 and 1980. The Treasury Department's *Monthly Statement of the Public Debt* was used to determine the relative quantities of government bonds of different maturities outstanding in those two years; and then maturities were converted into durations.

Table 3.A.1 gives the results of these calculations. The stock category included investment company shares plus other corporate equity plus equity in noncorporate business.

Duration data are not available on pension fund and life insurance reserves, which accounted for almost one-fifth of the financial net worth of households in both 1976 and 1980. We elected to compute asset weights under each of two assumptions—first, that these assets were spread evenly across durations 1–8 (the assumption used to allocate mortgages) and second, that they are predominantly long term. In the second case, we used the sum-of-the-years' digits method to allocate these assets triangularly across durations. The second case is probably more reasonable, inasmuch as pension reserve represents, for households, a long-term nominally

Table 3.A.1   Government Bond Weights

	1976		1980	
Duration	Corresponding Maturity (years)	Weight	Corresponding Maturity (years)	Weight
0	0– .25	.275	0– .25	.219
1	.25– 1.58	.357	.25– 1.60	.342
2	1.58– 2.65	.123	1.60– 2.75	.128
3	2.65– 4.00	.083	2.75– 4.20	.092
4	4.00– 5.45	.037	4.20– 5.75	.032
5	5.45– 7.13	.064	5.75– 7.80	.049
6	7.13– 8.80	.006	7.80–10.90	.031
7	8.80–10.60	.017	10.90–13.70	.021
8	10.60+	.036	13.70+	.097

Note: Flower bonds were omitted from the sample. The maturity date was taken to be first call date if the bond sold at a premium, and maturity otherwise.

Source: Weights by maturity from *Monthly Statement of the Public Debt,* May 1976, May 1980. Conversion to duration by using data on CRSP government bond files.

fixed claim. Table 3.A.2 reports results for both assumptions; the results reported in the body of the text are premised on the second assumption.

These market weights assume that the liabilities of financial intermediaries are treated as assets by the household sector, a coherent assumption under the finance paradigm. We also computed weights under the alternative assumption that financial intermediaries are a "veil," so that households behave as if they directly hold the assets of intermediaries.

The assumption that financial intermediaries are a veil results in a large redistribution of the weights from short- to long-term assets, while the weight on equity remains at the same level. Although the risk premiums on longer-term bonds rise appreciably, the overall pattern and levels of risk premiums remain much the same. For further details see Bodie et al. (1984).

3.A.1   Computing the Covariance Matrix

We first computed the expected real rate of return on Treasury bills by saying that the expected real yield over the coming month is the current nominal yield on a 30-day Treasury bill, i, less last month's inflation rate, π_{-1}:

$$R_0 = i - \pi_{-1}.$$

To obtain an initial covariance matrix, we used the covariance of the total rates of return for the 24 months before the month in which we started the procedure. In each succeeding month, the most recent unexpected returns were entered into the data matrix, and the previous 24 months of data were used to compute the covariance matrix. Thus, after the first 24

Table 3.A.2   Market Weights for the Household Sector

	Pension Fund Reserves Spread Evenly over Durations 1–8		Pension Fund Reserves Weighted toward High Durations	
	1976	1980	1976	1980
Stocks	.620	.640	.620	.640
Bonds: 0	.264	.262	.264	.262
1	.031	.026	.015	.007
2	.022	.017	.008	.003
3	.016	.013	.008	.005
4	.010	.007	.007	.005
5	.014	.009	.016	.012
6	.006	.007	.014	.016
7	.008	.006	.021	.020
8	.010	.013	.028	.032

months of the procedure, the covariance matrix was computed using only unexpected returns.

The entries in the covariance matrix were computed as

$$V_{ij}(T) = \frac{1}{24} \sum_{t=1}^{24} (R_{i,T-t} - \hat{R}_{i,T-t})(R_{j,T-1} - \hat{R}_{j,T-1}),$$

where R represents the realized real rate of return and $\hat{R}$ is the estimated expected real rate of return, computed using equation (1) and the previous month's covariance estimate.

An important advantage of this procedure is that the computed expected rates of return for each period are consistent with the model. The only part of this procedure which is ad hoc is the specification of the process generating expected rates of return on Treasury bills. The measure of covariance upon which the theory is based is the covariance of holding period rate of return deviations from expected rates of return. This is precisely what our procedure measures.

References

Bodie, A., Kane, A.; and McDonald, R. 1985. Inflation and the role of bonds in investor portfolios. In *Corporate Capital Structure in the United States*, edited by B. M. Friedman. Chicago: University of Chicago Press (for NBER).

———. 1984. Why haven't nominal rates declined? *Financial Analysts Journal* 40, no. 2 (March–April), 16–27.

Ibbotson, R. G., and Sinquefield, R. A. 1982. *Stocks, Bonds, Bills and Inflation: The Past and the Future*. Charlottesville, Va.: Financial Analysts Research Foundation.

Macaulay, F. R. 1938. *Some Theoretical Problems Suggested by the Movement of Interest Rates, Bond Yields, and Stock Prices in the U.S. since 1856*. New York: National Bureau of Economic Research, 1938.

Merton, R. C. 1980. On estimating the expected return on the market: an exploratory investigation. *Journal of Financial Economics* 8 (December), 323–61.

4 Implications of Government Deficits for Interest Rates, Equity Returns, and Corporate Financing

Benjamin M. Friedman

Corporate financial officers in the United States have traditionally regarded choices affecting their companies' debt-equity structures as central to the management of the modern business enterprise, and they have also recognized the critical importance for these choices of the market environment. The decision to issue new debt securities or new equity, and indeed the decision to raise external funds at all or to rely on internal equity additions, are key ways in which individual business corporations respond to the incentives and signals provided by the financial markets. These incentives, and the responses they call forth, are basic aspects of how the financial markets steer the allocation of the economy's scarce saving. In a fundamental sense, this process is a large part of why an economy like that of the United States has such highly developed capital markets in the first place.

A major new factor affecting the U.S. financial environment in the 1980s is the need to finance federal government budget deficits far in excess of any prior U.S. peacetime experience. Federal expenditures exceeded federal revenues by more than $100 billion for the first time during the recession year 1982, and the budget gap widened to nearly $200 billion, or 6% of the nation's gross national product, as the business expansion be-

Benjamin M. Friedman is professor of economics at Harvard University and program director for financial markets and monetary economics at the National Bureau of Economic Research. The author is grateful to Jeffrey Fuhrer for research assistance and helpful discussions and to Jeffrey Frankel and Lawrence Summers for useful comments on and corrections to an earlier draft.

gan in 1983. The limited narrowing of the deficit to about $170 billion in 1984, despite the continuing vigorous economic expansion, first represented the emergence of unprecedentedly large deficits on a high-employment basis as well. Prospects for the remainder of the 1980s depend both on the economy's further expansion and on future legislative action, of course, but a significant shrinking of the federal deficit before the end of the decade is problematic at best.[1]

Because of the central role of the market environment in affecting corporate financial decisions, this dramatic change in the stance of U.S. fiscal policy bears potentially significant implications not only for market interest rates but also for corporate financing, and hence for the quantity and allocation of physical capital formation undertaken by the U.S. business sector overall. In assessing these impacts, it is essential at the outset to judge the effects of continuing large government deficits on the structure of interest rates and equity returns confronting individual business corporations. That structure of asset returns depends, in turn, on the portfolio behavior of investors who collectively must hold whatever securities corporations, the government, and other borrowers may issue.

When investors are averse to bearing risk, as most investors plausibly are, their willingness to hold different kinds of securities depends on their assessments of the respective risks to which holding these securities exposes them. Investors typically prefer assets that they expect to bear higher returns when the associated risks are equivalent, but excessive risk can lead investors to shun even assets that they expect to bear very large returns. Similarly, investors' willingness to treat some kinds of securities as substitutes for others in their portfolios depends on the relationships that investors perceive among the associated risks to holding these securities as well as others. If two assets expose holders to essentially the same set of risks—to inflation, for example, or to the price of some raw commodity like oil or copper—investors typically treat the two as close substitutes and allocate their portfolios accordingly.

The object of the research summarized in this paper is to determine, on the basis of the plausible behavior of investors in the U.S. financial markets, how the emergence of continuing large federal government deficits at high employment is likely to affect the market environment for corporate financing. In particular, the specific question addressed here is how issues of either short- or long-term debt, to finance the government deficit, affect the structure of market returns on both debt and equity securities. Because investors' perceptions of risks on these various assets are unobserv-

---

1. Successive budget projections issued by the Office of Management and Budget and by the Congressional Budget Office differ; but most show that, in the absence of significant legislative action, the deficit will remain about 5% of gross national product.

able, and hence must be indirectly inferred from data describing information that investors presumably have, the approach taken here is to examine the answers to this question generated by several different ways of representing the all-important risk perceptions.

Section 4.1 briefly reviews the relationship between investors' demands for various assets and the respective risks that they associate with these assets. An aspect of this relationship that is of crucial importance in the context of the question addressed here is that not just the magnitude but even the direction of the effect of government bond issues on debt and equity returns is an empirical question, not answerable on the basis of theory alone. Sections 4.2, 4.3, and 4.4 present evidence on this question based on three different methods of inferring investors' risk perceptions from available data. Section 4.5 summarizes the conclusions implied by these three forms of evidence and calls attention to several important caveats.

To anticipate, the evidence presented here consistently indicates that financing government deficits by issuing short-term debt lowers the return on long-term debt, and lowers the return on equity by even more, in relation to the benchmark of the return on short-term debt; and that issuing long-term debt raises the return on long-term debt, and lowers the return on equity, again in relation to the benchmark of the return on short-term debt. Hence either form of deficit financing alters the structure of returns so as to render equity a more attractive form of finance from the issuer's perspective. This conclusion emerges from all three ways of inferring investors' risk perceptions considered here.

4.1   Government Debt Issues and Debt and Equity Returns

In light of the radical change in U.S. fiscal policy that occurred at the outset of the 1980s, it is important to know what effects the financing of government budget deficits has on the structure of asset returns. The U.S. government's budget deficit has become unprecedentedly large—even on a high-employment basis—in comparison to the economy's gross national product, to its supply of private saving, and to the ordinary financing requirements of business corporations and households. In the absence of a change from current tax and spending policies, this trend appears likely to continue. In addition, for the first time ever in U.S. peacetime experience, the federal government's outstanding debt is rising, steadily and rapidly, in comparison to gross national product. This trend too appears likely to continue for some time.

If these trends do continue, then the amount, and probably also the composition, of both business and household financing will be different in the 1980s than in previous cyclically comparable periods. From the perspective of the balance of saving and investment, only a half-again increase in the economy's net private saving rate would be sufficient to accommodate government deficits of the current magnitude plus the usual amount of private sector investment.[2] Similarly, because the economy's total of government plus private sector debt outstanding has typically been a stable multiple of gross national product, a rising government debt ratio suggests that private sector borrowers will not be able to increase their outstanding debt in pace with economic growth.[3]

To what extent—indeed, whether—government deficit financing "crowds out" private financing, and hence private capital formation, depends in the first instance on how deficit financing affects the market returns on private securities.[4] Neither corporations nor individuals voluntarily borrow less, or issue fewer equities (or retain less earnings), out of any innate desire to make the national accounts balance. Instead, private financing decisions depend on incentives and disincentives provided by market returns. Lower required rates of return (higher securities prices) presumably encourage borrowers and equity issuers, but higher required returns (lower securities prices) discourage private financing. Changes in the structure of relative returns—for example, between debt and equity— provide incentives to issue more of one kind of security and less of another.

How market returns respond to such developments as issues of government debt depends, in turn, on how investors perceive the risks associated with different kinds of securities. For any given set of risk assessments that market participants hold—including not just the riskiness of each asset individually but, importantly, the set of relationships connecting the risk on any one asset to that on any other—investors choose what assets to hold on the basis of the respective returns they expect various assets to bear. One pattern of expected returns will lead investors to allocate their portfolios in one way, while an alternative pattern of expected returns will lead them to choose a different allocation. No one investor ever holds all of the various assets available in the market, of course, but collectively all investors together must allocate their aggregate portfolio in just the composition corresponding to the assets outstanding in the market as a whole.

2. The U.S. economy's net private saving rate has been roughly steady at about 7% of gross national product for decades. (Thus far during the 1980s it has averaged less than 6%, but this decline was probably a result of the 1981–82 business recession.) The federal government deficit averaged less than 1% of gross national product in the 1950s and 1960s and less than 2% in the 1970s.

3. See Friedman (1982) for a discussion of the long-run behavior of the U.S. economy's debt-income ratio. The typical value for this ratio is about 1.45. The ratio normally rises modestly during recession, but the increase during 1981–82 was larger than usual. What has been even more unusual about the most recent business cycle is that the ratio did not promptly decline toward 1.45 during the recovery, and the ratio still remained above 1.60 at midyear 1985. As of the time of writing, it is too soon to determine whether this atypical debt issuing behavior represents a lasting break from prior experience.

4. For a formal presentation of the ideas at issue here, see Friedman (1978). The discussion both there and here is much in the spirit of Tobin (1961, 1969).

Under most circumstances, only one unique pattern of expected returns will lead all investors collectively to choose exactly that allocation of their aggregate portfolio.

When the composition of the assets outstanding in the market changes, therefore, the pattern of expected asset returns must change also, shifting to whatever configuration will induce investors collectively to hold exactly this new composition of assets. In this way, changes in the composition of assets outstanding—for example, as a result of government deficit financing—bring about changes in the market-clearing structure of expected asset returns. Moreover, because the economic function of these changes in expected returns is to induce investors to change their portfolio allocations, and because investors' demands for different assets depend on their perception of the associated risks, what changes in expected returns follow from any specific change in the composition of outstanding assets also depends on investors' risk perceptions.

Under most circumstances, increasing the market supply of any specific asset raises that asset's market-clearing expected return.[5] If expected returns did not change at all, investors would have to hold "too much" of the asset with increased supply. Their efforts to "trade out of" that asset depress its price and raise its subsequent expected return.

By contrast, an increase in the supply of any one asset may either raise or lower the expected return on any other asset. As that one asset's expected return rises, the expected returns on assets that investors regard as close substitutes for it—for example, government debt and high-grade corporate debt of comparable maturity—will rise in step. If investors are trying to trade out of the asset with increased supply, however, they must be trying to trade into something else, presumably assets that they do not regard as close substitutes for the asset with increased supply. Investors' efforts to trade into such other assets bid up their respective prices, so that their respective expected returns fall rather than rise.

This distinction, based on whether investors regard different securities as close or distant substitutes, and hence based on the risks that investors associate with holding different assets, is crucial to the question whether government deficit financing "crowds out" private capital formation. Forcing investors collectively to absorb into their aggregate portfolio an increased supply of government debt presumably raises the market-clearing expected return on government debt and on closely similar corporate debt instruments. Whether it raises or lowers the expected return on equity, or the expected return on dissimilar debt instruments, depends on the relative substitutabilities among debt, equity, and other classes of assets in investors' portfolios.

5. It necessarily does so when all assets are (imperfect) substitutes in investors' portfolios, and for plausible values of the relevant parameters it may do so even when some assets are complements.

If government deficit financing raises the expected returns on both debt and equity, its economic effect is to reduce incentives for corporate financing in any form (unless, of course, the additional government spending or reduced taxes increase expected profits, as would be expected when the economy's resources are less than fully employed). In this case deficit financing would indeed crowd out corporate capital formation and would have uncertain effects on the composition of the remaining (smaller) amount of corporate financing.

Alternatively, if government deficit financing raises the expected return on debt but lowers the expected return on equity, it changes the incentives for corporate financing in importantly different ways. In this case, the deficit financing would give corporations a clear incentive to substitute equity financing (including retentions) for debt financing. Whether it would crowd out or "crowd in" overall corporate financing, and hence overall corporate capital formation, depends on the relative magnitudes of the induced movements in debt and equity returns, as well as on the relative shares of debt and equity in the resulting overall corporate financing package.

The evidence examined here, based on the relative substitutabilities among short-term debt, long-term debt, and equity that follow from these three assets' respective risk properties, cannot by itself answer the question to what extent do the returns on all assets together rise in response to government deficit financing. Such movements of the overall return structure depend not only on relative asset substitutabilities but also on monetary policy, which lies beyond the scope of this paper.

The evidence examined here does show how the returns on specific assets move in relation to one another, however. In particular, the evidence presented in sections 4.2, 4.3, and 4.4 below consistently indicates that government deficit financing lowers the expected return on equity in comparison to the expected return on either short- or long-term debt. Moreover, this relative reduction of the equity return consistently emerges regardless of whether the government finances its deficit by issuing short- or long-term debt.

4.2   Evidence Based on Simple Inspection of Returns[6]

Individual investors, either on their own or through intermediaries, are the ultimate holders of the great majority of all corporate and government securities issued in the United States. Table 4.1 indicates the composition of the aggregate portfolio of financial assets held directly by U.S. households, as of year-end 1980, arranged according to three major asset classes

---

6. See Friedman (1985) for the details of the specific procedures underlying the results summarized in this section.

Table 4.1   Three-Class Disaggregation of Household Sector Financial Assets

Asset Class		1980:IV Value
Short-term debt (S):		$1,777.0
Money	268.0	
Regulated-return time and saving deposits	624.7	
Competitive-return time deposits	669.7	
Money market fund shares	74.4	
U.S. government securities	102.0	
Open market paper	38.2	
Long-term debt (L):		464.3
U.S. government securities	180.2	
State and local government obligations	74.2	
Corporate and foreign bonds	86.9	
Mortgages	122.5	
Equity (E):		1,215.6
Mutual fund shares	63.7	
Directly held equity shares	1,151.8	
Total		$3,456.9

Notes: Values in billions of dollars.
Detail may not add to total because of rounding.
Source: Board of Governors of the Federal Reserve System.

that differ from one another according to the risks associated with hold-ing them. *Short-term debt* includes all assets bearing real returns that are risky, over a single year or calendar quarter, only because of uncertainty about inflation. By contrast, *long-term debt* is risky because of uncertainty not only about inflation but also about changes in asset prices directly re-flecting changes in market interest rates. Similarly, *equity* is risky because of uncertainty about inflation and about changes in stock prices.

The first column of table 4.2 shows the per annum mean nominal return borne by each of these three classes of assets during 1960–80, including percentage capital gains or losses on both long-term debt and equity.[7] After allowance for what proved to be capital losses on average, over two decades in which interest rate levels typically were rising, the return on long-term debt differed only trivially from that on short-term debt despite a typically upward-sloping yield curve. As is familiar, the return on equity was substantially greater than on either maturity of debt.

The returns that investors ultimately care about, however, are not these observed nominal returns but the corresponding returns after both infla-

7. The nominal returns associated with these real returns are zero for money; a weighted average yield for time and savings deposits; the 4–6-month prime commercial paper yield for other short-term debt; the Moody's Baa corporate bond yield, plus annualized percentage capital gains or losses inferred by applying the consol pricing formula to changes in the Baa yield, for long-term debt; and the dividend-price yield, plus annualized percentage capital gains or losses on the Standard & Poor's 500 index, for equity.

Table 4.2   Mean Returns on Financial Assets, 1960–80

	Historical Means			Forecast Mean
	Nominal Before-Tax Return (%)	Real Before-Tax Return (%)	Real After-Tax Return (%)	Real After-Tax Return (%)
Short-term debt (r_S)	3.81	−1.62	−2.80	−2.40
Long-term debt (r_L)	3.83	−1.60	−3.83	−4.40
Equity (r_E)	10.64	5.21	3.13	3.73

Note: Values in percent per annum.

tion and taxes. The second column of table 4.2 shows the mean real returns on these three assets, calculated in each case by simply subtracting the per annum change in the consumer price index. Only equity bore a positive real return on average during these years. The third column of the table shows the corresponding mean after-tax real return on each asset, calculated by applying the household sector's average effective marginal tax rates in each year for interest, dividends, and capital gains to the respective nominal components of the before-tax returns.[8] Only equity bore a positive real after-tax return on average during this period. Moreover, because of the differential tax rates applicable to interest payments and capital gains (which, for bonds, were capital losses on average), the mean after-tax real return on long-term debt was about 1% per annum more negative than that on short-term debt.

The crucial aspect of these returns that determines the effect of government deficit financing is the set of risks investors associate with holding various assets. These perceptions presumably bear at least some relationship to the actual experience of asset returns over time. The heavy solid lines in the three panels of figure 4.1 plot the quarter-by-quarter experience of the annualized after-tax real returns on these three broad classes of assets during 1960–80. Because of the greater volatility of long-term debt and especially equity returns, the three panels are drawn with different scales.

The return on short-term debt, plotted in the top panel of the figure, experienced some volatility over this period, but its chief characteristic was a general downward trend after the mid-1960s due to the taxation of nominal rather than real interest payments. The return on long-term debt, plotted in the middle panel, experienced much more volatility, together with a modest overall downward trend. The major bond market swings during

8. The marginal tax rates applied to interest and dividends are values estimated by Estrella and Fuhrer (1983), on the basis of Internal Revenue Service data, to reflect the marginal tax bracket of the average recipient of these two respective kinds of income in each year. The marginal tax rate applied to capital gains is an analogous estimate, including allowances for deferral and loss offset features, due to Feldstein et al. (1983).

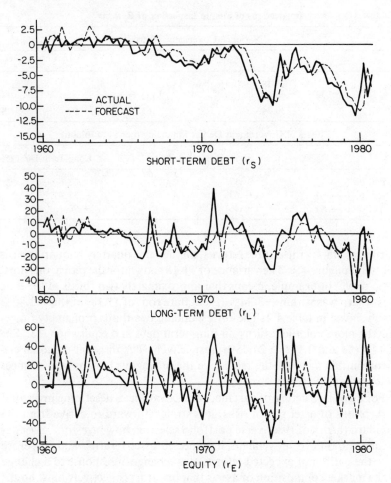

Fig. 4.1 Actual returns and regression-based forecasts, 1960–80

this period, including the "credit crunches" and subsequent rallies in 1966, 1970, and 1974, the reaction to the Federal Reserve System's new monetary policy procedures in 1979, and the imposition of credit controls in 1980, are readily visible. The return on equity, plotted in the bottom panel, experienced still more volatility and again a modest downward trend. The period's major stock market swings are also readily visible, including the crash in 1962, the response to the 1966 and 1970 "credit crunches," and especially the response to the combination of credit crunch and OPEC in 1974.

Even a casual inspection of figure 4.1 indicates that the returns on these three broad classes of assets tend to move together over time, and it is plausible that investors are aware of these comovements in at least some respects. The upper panel of table 4.3 shows the actual variances and co-

Table 4.3   Implications of Simple Inspection of Returns

Variance-Covariance Matrix

	r_S	r_L	r_E
r_S	11.18		
r_L	29.91	209.35	
r_E	30.24	161.77	597.86

Effects of Government Deficit Financing (per $100 Billion)

	Short-Term Debt (%)	Long-Term Debt (%)
Effect on $(r_L - r_S)$	−.17	.22
Effect on $(r_E - r_S)$	−.63	−.35
Effect on $(r_E - r_L)$	−.46	−.57

variances among these three returns, on the same quarter-by-quarter basis plotted in figure 4.1. The variance of 11.18 shown for the return on short-term debt, for example, means that approximately two-thirds of the time this return was within ± 3.34% (the square root of 11.18) of the − 2.80% mean shown in table 4.2. The corresponding two-thirds probability ranges for the more volatile returns on long-term debt and equity are − 3.18% ± 14.47% and 3.13% ± 24.45%, respectively. The three off-diagonal elements in this panel of the table give the analogous pairwise covariances among the three assets.

For a given structure of variances and covariances describing investors' perceptions of asset return risks, it is straightforward to derive from the standard theory of risk-averse portfolio selection how investors' asset demands respond to movements in expected asset returns, and therefore how the pattern of expected returns must change in response to a change in the market composition of assets that investors collectively must hold.[9] The lower panel of table 4.3 summarizes the effects of government deficit financing, on the specific assumption that the variances and covariances reported above, simply calculated from the observed experience of asset returns during 1960–80, describe investors' risk perceptions. Because the effects of government deficit financing depend on what kind of securities the Treasury issues,[10] the table reports separate sets of effects following from changes in the respective supplies of short- and long-term debt.

9. The specific assumption made throughout this paper is that investors' behavior exhibits constant relative risk aversion, with value equal to four. Bodie et al. (1985) also assumed constant relative risk aversion equal to four. This value is about in the middle of the range of available empirical estimates. (Friend and Blume [1975] suggested a value in excess of two, Grossman and Shiller [1981] suggested four, and Friend and Hasbrouck [1982] suggested six.) See Friedman (1985) for details of the calculations.

10. More precisely, the effects depend on issues by the Treasury less net purchases by the Federal Reserve System.

If the Treasury finances a deficit by issuing short-term debt, the expected return on short-term debt presumably rises in comparison to the expected returns on other assets.[11] Put the other way around, in this case the expected returns on other assets fall in comparison to that on short-term debt. Which other assets' returns fall by more and which by less depends on the relative asset substitutabilities that depend, in turn, on investors' risk perceptions. The results shown in table 4.3 indicate that the expected differential between the returns on long- and short-term debt (which is presumably positive on the basis of past experience) narrows by .17%, while the expected differential between the returns on equity and short-term debt (also presumably positive) narrows by .63%, in response to each $100 billion additional supply of short-term government debt to be held in investors' aggregate portfolio. In other words, if the short-term debt return is held fixed by monetary policy, the expected returns on long-term debt and equity *fall* by .17% and .63%, respectively. The expected differential between the returns on equity and long-term debt (also presumably positive) therefore narrows by .46%. For a $200 billion deficit, the effects are exactly double these magnitudes.

Similarly, if the Treasury finances a deficit by issuing long-term debt, the expected return on long-term debt presumably rises in comparison to the expected returns on other assets. If the short-term debt return is fixed, the long-term debt return then rises absolutely and the returns on other assets may either rise or fall. Which other assets' returns rise and which fall again depends on relative asset substitutabilities, and hence on investors' perceptions of risk. The results shown in table 4.3 indicate that the differential between the returns on long- and short-term debt widens by .22%, while the expected differential between the returns on equity and short-term debt narrows by .35%, in response to each $100 billion additional supply of long-term debt. In other words, if the return on short-term debt is fixed, the expected return on long-term debt *rises* by .22% and the expected return on equity *falls* by .35%. The expected differential between the returns on equity and long-term debt therefore again narrows, in this case by .57%. Once again, for a $200 billion deficit the effects would be twice as large.

The finding that financing the government deficit by either short- or long-term debt lowers the expected return on equity, in comparison to the expected returns on both classes of debt instruments, bears potentially important implications for corporate financing. Nevertheless, these estimated effects directly depend on the assumed underlying variance-covariance structure, and simply using the observed historical pattern of asset return movements to represent investors' perceptions presumably overstates the amount of uncertainty investors actually attach to their expectations of

11. See again the discussion in sec. 4.1, esp. n. 5.

uncertain asset returns. Although the emphasis here is on the direction rather than the magnitude of the effects of government deficit financing, incorrectly represented risk perceptions may lead not just to incorrect estimated magnitudes but to incorrect inferences about direction as well. Some more satisfactory representation of investors' risk perceptions is clearly needed.

4.3   Evidence Based on Continually Updated Forecasting Regressions[12]

The simple procedure used in section 4.2 to represent investors' risk perceptions suffers from attributing to investors both too little information and, for some applications, too much. As long as the object of the analysis is to describe investors' behavior at any time after year-end 1980, it is satisfactory to assume that investors know the actual experience of asset return means, variances, and covariances during 1960–80. By contrast, if the goal is to describe investors' behavior on average during this period, then the procedure used in section 4.2 attributes to investors information which they did not have at the outset but gradually acquired as time passed.

This procedure also attributes too little information to investors by disregarding their knowledge, at each point in time, of the most recent realizations of security returns and the principal determinants of these returns. During the 1960–80 period the after-tax real returns on all three classes of assets considered here exhibited substantial serial correlation because the underlying movements of inflation, interest rates, and stock prices were themselves serially correlated.[13] When returns are serially correlated over time, information about the most recent actual values is a useful ingredient in forming expectations about returns in the immediate future. Ignoring that information can lead to excessively large estimates of the uncertainty surrounding these expectations, as is apparently the problem with the results presented in table 4.3. Table 4.4 presents a set of analogous results based on a procedure that takes much more careful account of what information investors did and did not have at any particular time.

As of the beginning of each calendar quarter, investors presumably know the stated interest rates on short-term debt instruments, the current prices and the coupon rates on long-term debt instruments, the current prices and (approximately) the dividends on equities, and the relevant tax rates. The three uncertain elements that they must forecast over the com-

---

12. See Friedman (1984) for the details of the specific procedures underlying the results summarized in this section.

13. The first-order serial correlation coefficients are .86 for the short-term debt return, .51 for the long-term debt return, and .33 for the equity return. Corresponding coefficients for inflation, bond capital gains, and equity capital gains are .90, .44, and .31, respectively.

Table 4.4   Implications of Continually Updated Forecasting Regressions

Variance-Covariance Matrix

	r_S	r_L	r_E
r_S	1.25		
r_L	3.62	76.61	
r_E	6.45	48.09	317.27

Effects of Government Deficit Financing (per $100 Billion)

	Short-Term Debt (%)	Long-Term Debt (%)
Effect on $(r_L - r_S)$	$-.06$	.10
Effect on $(r_E - r_S)$	$-.33$	$-.24$
Effect on $(r_E - r_L)$	$-.27$	$-.34$

ing quarter, in order to form expectations of the after-tax real returns on the three broad classes of assets considered here, are inflation, the capital gain or loss due to changing bond prices, and the capital gain or loss due to changing stock prices.

The procedure underlying the results reported in table 4.4 represents investors as forming expectations of these three uncertain return elements, at each point in time, by estimating a linear regression model relating each element to past values of itself and the other two, using all data observed through the immediately preceding period. In addition to providing forecast values of the three uncertain elements for the period ahead, the linear regression model at each point in time also directly indicates the variances and covariances associated with the forecasts derived in this way. After each period elapses, investors can then repeat the same procedure, incorporating the one new observation on inflation and on long-term debt and equity capital gains into the data used to reestimate the linear regression model to make forecasts for the next period.

Given the simple arithmetic connection between asset returns and these underlying uncertain elements, and given investors' presumed knowledge of the other elements comprising returns, these 1-period-ahead forecasts of inflation and the respective capital gains on long-term debt and equity directly imply 1-period-ahead forecasts of the after-tax real returns on all three classes of assets at each point in time. Similarly, the variances and covariances associated with the forecasts of inflation and the two capital gains directly imply the variances and covariances associated with the corresponding forecasts of the three asset returns. The key advantage of representing investors' expectations in this way, in contrast to the simple procedure used in section 4.2, lies in focusing strictly on information that investors actually had at each point in time and in making a not implausible assumption about how they might have used it.

The heavy solid lines in the three panels of figure 4.2 show the quarter-by-quarter movements, during 1960–80, of the per annum rates of inflation, capital gains on long-term debt, and capital gains on equity. (As in fig. 4.1, the scales differ.) The corresponding broken lines plot the successive 1-period-ahead forecasts generated by this continually updated linear regression procedure, for each quarter during this 21-year period. For 1960:I the three forecasts are based on the linear regression model relating each uncertain element to a constant term, four lagged values of itself, and four lagged values of each of the other two uncertain elements, estimated using data for 1953:II–1959:IV. For 1960:II the procedure is the same except that the data used to estimate the linear regression model cover

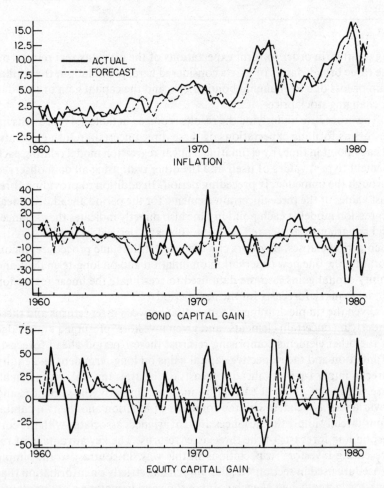

Fig. 4.2   Actual elements of returns and regression-based forecasts, 1960–80

1953:II–1960:I. The procedure is analogous for subsequent periods, ending with the use of data for 1953:II–1980:III to generate the 1-period-ahead forecasts for 1980:IV.

The degree of success achieved by these 1-period-ahead forecasts naturally varies according to the extent of the serial correlation in the series being forecast. The simple correlation between the actual outcomes and the corresponding forecasts derived in this way is .88 for inflation, .42 for long-term debt capital gains, and .23 for equity capital gains. As is clear from the figure, this inherently backward-looking forecast procedure enjoys the advantages, and suffers the shortcomings, of expecting the immediate future to be like the immediate past.

The broken lines in the three panels of figure 4.1 plot the successive 1-period-ahead forecasts of the three after-tax real returns corresponding to these forecasts of the underlying uncertain elements. Here, too, the backward-looking procedure represents the immediate future as resembling the immediate past, so that the success achieved by the forecasts varies according to the serial correlation in the different asset returns. The simple correlation between the actual returns and the corresponding forecasts is .83 for short-term debt, .51 for long-term debt, and .30 for equities. The final column of table 4.2 shows the 1960–80 means of these 1-period-ahead forecasts of the three after-tax real returns. Comparison with the actual means shown in the immediately preceding column indicates that, on average, these forecasts were somewhat too optimistic about the returns on short-term debt and equity and somewhat too pessimistic about the return on long-term debt.

The upper panel of table 4.4 shows the variances and covariances associated with these three asset return forecasts, on average for 1960–80.[14] These values are much smaller than those shown in table 4.3, indicating the importance of investors' having (and using) information about recent actual returns. The two-thirds probability ranges for the three after-tax real returns are ±1.12% for short-term debt, ±8.75% for long-term debt, and ±17.81% for equity.

The lower panel of table 4.4 shows the implied effects of government deficit financing that follow from assuming that the variances and covariances shown above represent investors' perceptions of the risks associated with the respective returns on these three broad classes of assets. As is to be expected, the smaller uncertainty than in table 4.3 makes investors more readily willing to reallocate their portfolios in response to any given movement of expected asset returns, and therefore reduces (in absolute value) the movement of returns needed to induce investors collectively to accommodate a given change in the composition of assets to be held. Even

---

14. The values shown are the simple means of the variances and covariances for each of the 84 quarters.

so, the estimated effects are hardly negligible. For example, for the expected differential between the returns on equity and long-term debt, the difference between a $200 billion deficit and a balanced budget is .54% under short-term financing and .68% under long-term financing.

In each case the direction of the implied effect shown in table 4.4 is identical to that shown in table 4.3. Financing government deficits by issuing short-term debt lowers the return on long-term debt, and lowers the return on equity by even more, in comparison to the return on short-term debt. Financing deficits by issuing long-term debt raises the return on long-term debt and lowers the return on equity, again in comparison to the return on short-term debt. Under either form of deficit financing, therefore, the return on equity falls in comparison to the return on debt securities of either maturity.

4.4   Implications of Survey Expectations

Because the risk perceptions that determine the effects of government deficit financing are inherently unobservable, so that any procedure for representing them is necessarily only tentative, it makes sense to examine the implications of several different representations rather than rely on only one. Opinion surveys provide a further source of information about what investors thought at specific times in the past. Although the available surveys typically just ask respondents to forecast specific economic variables, without also asking for them to state the uncertainty that they associate with their forecasts, it is nevertheless possible to use survey expectations to infer perceptions of uncertainty in a variety of ways.

The upper panel of table 4.5 summarizes the forecasting performance of the Livingston survey of inflation and stock price expectations, and the Goldsmith-Nagan survey of long-term interest rate expectations, by

Table 4.5   Mean Survey Expectations, 1969:IV–1980:IV

Expected Asset Return Components		
	Historical Mean (%)	Survey Mean (%)
Inflation	7.94	5.87
Aaa bond yield	8.95	8.74
S&P stock price index	98.77	108.14

Implied Expected Real After-Tax Returns		
	Historical Mean (%)	Survey Mean (%)
Short-term debt (r_S)	−4.86	−2.78
Long-term debt (r_L)	−1.97	4.03
Equity (r_E)	.44	28.36

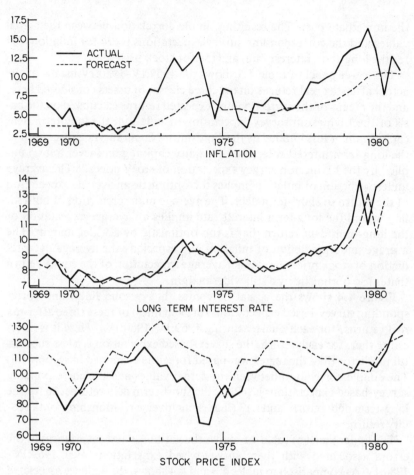

Fig. 4.3   Actual elements of returns and survey-based forecasts, 1969–
                      80

showing the survey means and the corresponding actual means for
1969:IV–1980:IV.[15] On average, the Livingston respondents underpredicted inflation and overpredicted stock prices by substantial margins,
while the Goldsmith-Nagan respondents only modestly underpredicted
the long-term interest rate. Figure 4.3 shows these actual outcomes (heavy
solid lines) and the corresponding survey expectations (broken lines) for
each quarter during this period. Especially for the long-term interest rate,
but to some extent for inflation and stock prices as well, survey respondents typically did forecast the immediate future as if it would resemble

15. The first Goldsmith-Nagan survey took place in September 1969. The Livingston data
are available for a much longer period. I am grateful to Peter Nagan for providing his un-
published data for use in this and other research.

the immediate past. The resulting simple correlation between the actual values and the corresponding survey expectations is .74 for inflation, .84 for the long-term interest rate, and .50 for stock prices.

The lower panel of table 4.5 shows the 1969:IV–1980:IV means of the actual after-tax real returns on the three classes of assets considered here, and the means of the corresponding expected returns calculated on the basis of the Livingston survey expectation of inflation, the long-term debt capital gain or loss implied by the Goldsmith-Nagan survey expectation of the long-term interest rate, and the equity capital gain (never a loss) implied by the Livingston survey expectation of stock prices.[16] The average underprediction of inflation implies too optimistic an average expectation of the return to short-term debt. The average underprediction of both inflation and the long-term interest rate implies an average expectation of the long-term debt return that is too optimistic by a wider margin. The average underprediction of inflation and especially the average overprediction of stock prices implies an average expectation of the equity return that is too optimistic by a still wider margin.

Figure 4.4 shows the actual outcomes (heavy solid lines) and corresponding survey-based expectations (broken lines) of these three after-tax real returns, for each quarter during 1969:IV–1980:IV.[17] Here it is interesting that, for each return, the survey-based expectation is a less successful predictor than the regression-based forecasts examined in section 4.3. The simple correlation between the actual values and the corresponding survey-based expectations is .62 for the short-term debt return, .26 for the long-term debt return, and -.13 (that is, an inverse relationship) for the equity return.

The upper panel of table 4.6 shows the variances and covariances of the errors associated with these survey-based expectations over 1969:IV–1980:IV. As comparison to tables 4.3 and 4.4 shows, the variance associated with the return on short-term debt here is smaller than that implied by the simple inspection procedure used in section 4.2, but larger than that implied by the regression procedure in section 4.3. The two-thirds probability range for the short-term debt return is ±2.49%. By contrast, the respective variances associated with the returns on long-term debt and equity are larger than the corresponding variances implied by either the simple inspection procedure or the regression procedure. The two-thirds

16. Once again, as of the beginning of each period investors presumably know the stated interest rates on short-term debt instruments, the current prices and coupons on long-term debt instruments, and the current prices and dividends on equity. For short-term debt and equity, the actual returns here are the same as those analyzed in secs. 4.2 and 4.3. For long-term debt the return is based on the Aaa utility rate used in the Goldsmith-Nagan survey, rather than on the Baa corporate rate as in secs. 4.2 and 4.3.

17. It is necessary to interpolate quarterly values of the inflation and stock price expectations because the Livingston survey asks for 6-month-ahead expectations twice per year. (The Goldsmith-Nagan survey asks for 3-month-ahead expectations four times per year.)

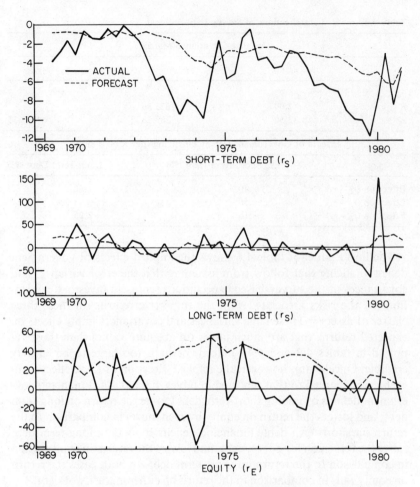

Fig. 4.4 Actual returns and survey-based forecasts, 1969–80

probability ranges are ± 32.80% and ± 36.50% for the long-term debt return and the equity return, respectively.[18] Asset returns were more volatile on average during the 1970s than they were during the 1960s (and hence, on average, during 1960–80), but the major part of the explanation for the larger variances shown in table 4.6 is the weaker correlations between the survey expectations and the corresponding actual outcomes.[19]

18. The error variance for the return on long-term debt is dominated by the sharp drop in the Aaa (new issue) rate when credit controls were imposed in 1980:II. (The Baa seasoned rate, used in secs. 4.2 and 4.3, fell only slightly in 1980:II.) For the 1969:IV–1980:IV period omitting this one quarter, the corresponding error variance is 687.52.

19. The variances for 1969:IV–1980:IV, computed as in table 4.3, are (from upper left to lower right) 9.82, 293.90, and 763.33. The corresponding variances computed as in table 4.4 are 1.54, 89.97, and 353.64.

Table 4.6   Implications of Survey Expectations

Variance-Covariance Matrix

	r_S	r_L	r_E
r_S	6.22		
r_L	7.09	1075.86	
r_E	32.50	207.23	1332.35

Effects of Government Deficit Financing (per $100 billion)

	Short-Term Debt (%)	Long-Term Debt (%)
Effect on $(r_L - r_S)$	$-.40$	1.62
Effect on $(r_E - r_S)$	$-.56$	$-.63$
Effect on $(r_E - r_L)$	$-.16$	-2.25

The lower panel of table 4.6 shows the implied effects of government deficit financing that follow from assuming that the error variances and covariances of the survey-based expectations represent investors' perceptions of the risks associated with the respective returns on these three classes of assets.[20] These large variances and covariances imply effects on expected returns that are much larger (in absolute value) than those reported in tables 4.3 and 4.4—indeed, perhaps too large to be entirely credible. Once again, however, the implied direction of these effects is in each case identical to that reported in tables 4.3 and 4.4. Financing government deficits by issuing short-term debt lowers the return on long-term debt, and lowers the return on equity by even more, in comparison to the return on short-term debt. Financing deficits by issuing long-term debt raises the return on long-term debt, and lowers the return on equity, again in comparison to the return on short-term debt. In both cases the return on equity falls in comparison to the return on either maturity of debt.

4.5   Conclusions and Caveats

How the financing of government budget deficits affects the structure of expected asset returns depends on assets' relative substitutabilities in investors' aggregate portfolio, and these substitutabilities in turn depend on how investors perceive the risks associated with the respective asset returns. Increasing the supply that investors collectively must hold of any asset raises that asset's market-clearing expected return. By contrast, an

20. An alternative use of these survey data in this context would be to use each period's dispersion of individual survey responses to proxy that period's uncertainty. The potential shortcomings of assuming a relationship between dispersion among different individuals' point estimates and the uncertainty perceived by the representative individual are well known, however.

increase in the supply of any one asset may either raise or lower the expected return on any other asset.

The empirical results reported in this paper, based on three different ways of representing investors' risk perceptions, consistently indicate that government deficit financing raises expected debt returns relative to expected equity returns, regardless of the maturity of the government's financing. More specifically, financing government deficits by issuing short-term debt lowers the return on long-term debt, and lowers the return on equity by even more, relative to the return on short-term debt. Financing deficits by issuing long-term debt raises the return on long-term debt, but lowers the return on equity, again in comparison to the return on short-term debt. The indicated magnitudes of these effects differ according to the method used to represent investors' risk perceptions, but the qualitative results are consistent throughout. Moreover, many of the indicated magnitudes are large enough to matter economically.[21]

These results imply that continuing large government deficits at full employment lead to market incentives for individual business corporations to emphasize reliance on equity (including retentions), and reduce reliance on debt, in comparison with the composition of corporate financing that would prevail in the absence of the need to finance the government budget deficit. Because these results describe effects only on relative returns, rather than effects on absolute levels of returns, they answer questions about the composition of corporate financing but not about its total. Nevertheless, in conjunction with some further assumption to anchor the overall return structure—for example, that monetary policy accommodates the deficit so as to keep expected short-term real returns unchanged, or, alternatively, that monetary policy is not accommodative and hence lets expected short-term real returns rise if the deficit is large enough—these results also bear straightforward implications for the volume of corporate financing and, in turn, for corporate capital formation.

Finally, at least three caveats are potentially important in evaluating these results. First, as the discussion throughout this paper has repeatedly emphasized, investors' perceptions of asset risk are not directly observable. It is therefore necessary to use some operational procedure to represent them. It is significant that qualitatively identical results follow from each of the three quite different procedures used for this purpose here. Even so, no data-based procedure can ever represent investors' perceptions perfectly, and each of the three procedures used here may go astray in some way that matters importantly for the consequent results.

21. The magnitudes reported here are larger than those found by Frankel (forthcoming) in a study that in some respects parallels the work described here. One source of this difference is that Frankel assumed a risk aversion value of two, instead of four as assumed here. Another is that Frankel included tangible assets in household wealth (while still excluding all liabilities), instead of focusing only on financial assets as here.

The second caveat, also noted in the discussion above, is that the analysis in this paper focuses only on the financing effects associated with government deficits. The deficit is just the difference between government expenditures and tax revenues, however, and each has effects on nonfinancial economic activity. When the economy's resources are less then fully employed, greater expenditures and/or lower taxes stimulate real spending, incomes, and output. At full employment the chief result is inflation. In either case the associated nonfinancial effects of government deficits typically create indirect financial pressures that interact with the direct financing effects studied here.

The third caveat is that the analysis in this paper focuses only on financial assets and, since some 90% of all borrowing by U.S. households takes place to finance purchases of nonfinancial assets, ignores households' liabilities. Not taking household liabilities into account is probably not a major concern in the context of this paper's focus (it could be in other contexts), but the omission of nonfinancial assets potentially is. Whether two assets are close or distant substitutes can depend importantly on what other assets are also in the investor's portfolio, or at least available for purchase. Moreover, nonfinancial assets bulk large in households' aggregate portfolio. As of year-end 1980, U.S. households owned $2.8 trillion of residential real estate and $1.0 trillion of consumer durables—together more than the $3.5 trillion of financial assets shown in table 4.1. Including these nonfinancial assets and their returns in an analysis like that undertaken here is an important subject for further research.

References

Bodie, Z., Kane, A., and McDonald, R. 1985. Inflation and the role of bonds in investor portfolios. In Friedman, Benjamin M., ed., *Corporate capital structures in the United States*. Chicago: University of Chicago Press.

Estrella, A., and Fuhrer, J. 1983. Average effective marginal rates on interest and dividend income in the United States, 1960–1979. National Bureau of Economic Research. Mimeographed.

Feldstein, M., Poterba, J., and Dicks-Mireau, L. 1983. The effective tax rate and the pretax rate of return. *Journal of Public Economics* 21:129–58.

Frankel, J. A. Forthcoming. A test of portfolio crowding-out and other issues in finance. *Quarterly Journal of Economics*.

Friedman, B. M. 1978. Crowding out or crowding in? Economic consequences of financing government deficits. *Brookings Papers on Economic Activity:*593–641.

_____.1982. Debt and economic activity in the United States. In Friedman, B. M., ed., *The changing roles of debt and equity in financing U.S. capital formation.* Chicago: University of Chicago Press.

_____.1984. Crowding out or crowding in? Evidence on debt-equity substitutability. National Bureau of Economic Research. Mimeographed.

_____. 1985. The substitutability of debt and equity securities. In Friedman, Benjamin M., ed., *Corporate capital structures in the United States.* Chicago: University of Chicago Press.

Friend, I., and Blume, M. E. 1975. The demand for risky assets. *American Economic Review* 65:900–923.

Friend, I., and Hasbrouck, J. 1982. Effect of inflation on the profitability and valuation of U.S. corporations. In M. Sarnat and G. Szego, eds., *Savings, investment and capital markets in an inflationary economy.* Cambridge, Mass.: Ballinger.

Grossman, S. J., and Shiller, R. J. 1981. The determinants of the variability of stock market prices. *American Economic Review* 71:222–27.

Tobin, J. 1961. Money, capital and other stores of value. *American Economic Review* 51:26–37.

_____. 1969. A general equilibrium approach to monetary theory. *Journal of Money, Credit and Banking* 1:354–71.

5 Valuing Financial Flexibility

Scott P. Mason

5.1 Introduction

Two facts that corporations, underwriters, and investors have been forced to confront are increased capital market volatility and increased complexity in the design of securities. A seemingly endless list of new security ideas has compounded the already difficult problem of making sound issuance, underwriting, and investment decisions in highly volatile markets. However, these two facts, increased volatility and increased complexity, are not unrelated. Virtually all of the complexity in securities can be viewed as the inclusion of different options in a straight debt contract. Even such common debt features as call provisions and call protection can be viewed as options. The value of a call provision is the value of an option to redeem debt at a fixed price prior to maturity, and the value of call protection is the value of shortening the life of that option. Given the fact that the value of options is driven most significantly by volatility, the advantage of including options, that is, financial flexibility, in securities has increased with increased market volatility. This would appear to explain why corporate issuers and institutional investors have shown substantial interest in securities which improve their flexibility in volatile markets. In low-volatility markets, corporations and investors would not lose a great deal of flexibility if options were excluded from the design of securities and would not make large valuation errors if options were ignored in valuing securities. But given that options are more valuable in a volatile market, significant valuation errors could result from ignoring options or valuing them through possibly outdated rules of thumb. There-

Scott Mason is associate professor at the Graduate School of Business Administration, Harvard University, and a faculty research fellow at the National Bureau of Economic Research.

fore, techniques which can consistently reflect the role of volatility in the value of options or flexibility should be of interest to issuers, underwriters, and investors.

A major breakthrough in the valuation of options came in 1973 when Fisher Black and Myron Scholes presented a technique for valuing calls and puts written on common stock. While their findings had an immediate and significant impact on the stock option markets, Black and Scholes offered a qualitative insight which may prove of even greater practical significance than their famous quantitative formula: corporate liabilities and covenants can be viewed as combinations of simple option contracts. This generalization of option pricing models to corporate securities and covenants became known as Contingent Claims Analysis (CCA).

This paper summarizes the results of some research by Jones, Mason, and Rosenfeld (JMR) (1984) and presents some new results, which test the ability of a CCA model based on Black and Scholes's option pricing principles to predict the market price of callable corporate debt, and therefore, the price of such common debt covenants as call provisions and call protection. This research had its origin in some earlier work (JMR 1983) done for the National Bureau's conference on corporate capital structures in the United States. In addition, some numerical CCA results are reported which demonstrate the impact of changing interest rate volatility on the value of call provisions and call protection. First, however, the paper briefly reviews the basics of option pricing and demonstrates the significance of option pricing to pricing corporate securities and individual covenants.

5.2   Corporate Liabilities as Options[1]

To understand the relationship between corporate liabilities and options, consider first the most fundamental options: calls and puts. An American call option, whose price is denoted by C, gives its owner the right to purchase an asset, for example, one share of stock, with current price S, at an exercise price, X, on or before an expiration date which is T time periods from now. The call option owner will only exercise his right to buy if it is to his advantage. Figure 5.1 depicts the value of the call option as it depends on the stock price on the expiration date. Should the stock price on the expiration date be less than the exercise price, then the call option owner will not exercise his right to purchase the stock and the option will expire worthless, that is, $C = 0$. If, however, the stock price is greater than the exercise price, then the call option will be worth $S - X$, the difference between the stock price and the exercise price. An option is

---

1. This section of the paper borrows from Mason and Merton (1985), which more fully develops the concepts of corporate liabilities and covenants as options.

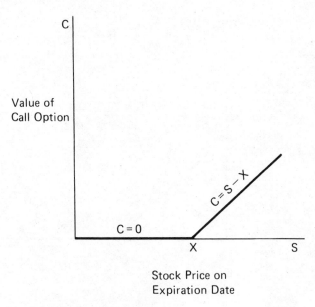

Fig. 5.1   Payoff to call option

termed "American" if it can be exercised on or before the expiration date and "European" if it can be exercised only on the expiration date.

Clearly, a call option pays off more the higher the underlying stock price at expiration. If the volatility of the stock increases, then the probability increases that the stock price will be higher at expiration. It is also true that an increase in volatility increases the probability that the stock price will be lower at expiration, but the effect of a lower stock price on the expected payoff to an option is bounded since the option holder has the right not to exercise—that is, not to surrender the exercise price—if it is not in his best interest. Therefore, increased volatility increases the expected payoff to the option and increases the option's value.

An American put option, P, gives its owner the right to sell one share of stock, S, at an exercise price, X, on or before its expiration date T periods from now. Again, the put option owner will only exercise his right to sell if it is to his advantage. Figure 5.2 depicts the value of the put option on its expiration date. If the stock price on the expiration date is greater than the exercise price, then the put option owner will not exercise his right to sell the stock and the put option will expire worthless, $P = 0$. However, should the stock price be less than the exercise price, then the put option owner will exercise his right to sell the stock and the put option will be worth $X - S$, the difference between the exercise price and the stock price. The expected payoff to the put also increases given increased volatility since the probability that the stock price will be lower increases and the put

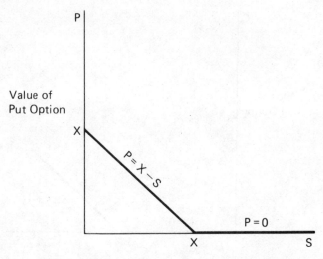

Fig. 5.2   Payoff to put option

owner need not exercise if it is not to his advantage, that is, if the stock price is above the exercise price.

An important relationship between European call and put prices can be derived from figures 5.1 and 5.2. Consider buying a European call and selling a European put on the same stock, with the same exercise price and expiration date. The net investment is

$$c - p.$$

The value of this investment position at expiration of the options is depicted in figure 5.3. The value of the investment position on the expiration date is $S - X$, the difference between the stock price and the exercise price. The investment can have negative value if the stock price is below the exercise price because the call will expire worthless and the put will be exercised against its seller. However, there is another investment position involving no options which can replicate the payoff depicted in figure 5.3. Consider buying one share of stock, S, borrowing on a discount basis X dollars for T time periods at rate r, that is, the proceeds from the loan will be $X(1 + r)^{-T}$ allowing for discounting. This second investment is then

$$S - X(1 + r)^{-T}.$$

In T periods the value of this position will be $S - X$, since the position owns one share of stock and owes X dollars. But, if these two positions have precisely the same value in T time periods, then it must be true that the initial net investment necessary to establish the positions is the same:

$$c - p = S - X(1 + r)^{-T}. \tag{1}$$

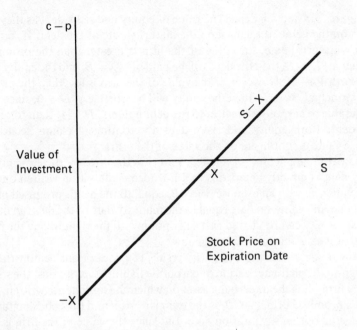

Fig. 5.3   Payoff to investment position

Expression (1) is known to professional traders as "put-call parity." The expression simply says that prices in the call, put, stock, and lending markets must be such that (1) is always true. If this were not the case, traders would simply buy the lower-priced alternative and sell the higher-priced alternative and earn an immediate riskless return on zero net investment.

With these fundamental options properties as background, the correspondence between options and corporate liabilities can now be established. Consider figure 5.4, the economic balance sheet of a simple firm which has only two liabilities: equity, E, and a single issue of zero-coupon debt, D, where the equity receives no dividends and the firm will issue no new securities while the debt is outstanding.

$$\frac{V}{V} \quad \Bigg| \quad \frac{\begin{array}{c} D \\ E \end{array}}{V}$$

Fig. 5.4   Firm's economic balance sheet

The left-hand side of the balance sheet represents the economic value, V, of the firm. The right-hand side lists the economic value of all the liabilities of the firm.

Figures 5.5 and 5.6 depict the value of equity and risky debt as they depend on the value of the firm on the maturity date of the debt. If, on the debt's maturity date, the value of the firm is greater than the promised principal, $V > B$, then the debt will be paid off, $D = B$, and the equity will be worth $V - B$. However, if the value of the firm is less than the promised principal, $V < B$, then the equity will be worthless, $E = 0$, since it is preferable to surrender the firm to the debt holders, $D = V$, than to repay the debt. Both equity and risky debt are contingent claims securities whose value is contingent on the value of the firm.

Now compare figures 5.1 and 5.5. Equity in the presence of zero-coupon risky debt is directly analogous to a European call option written on the firm value, V, with an exercise price, B, equal to the debt's promised principal and an expiration date equal to the maturity date of the debt. In other words, equity can be viewed as a call option with the right to buy the firm for B dollars T time periods from now.

Now return to the put-call parity result, (1), for options demonstrated earlier. In the characterization of corporate liabilities as options, the value of the firm, V, is the underlying asset on which the options are written; the debt's promised principal, B, is the exercise price; and the debt's maturity date is the option's expiration date. But since the value of the firm is the sum of the value of the equity and the value of the debt,

$$V = E + D,$$

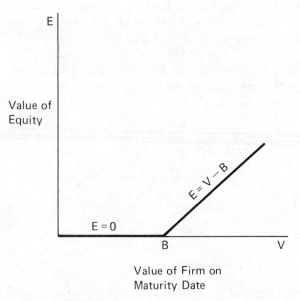

Fig. 5.5   Payoff to equity

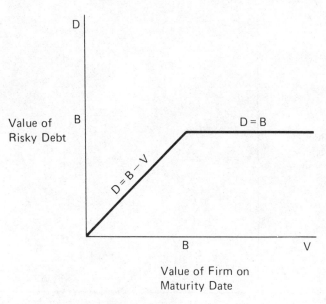

Fig. 5.6   Payoff to debt

and since the value of the equity is analogous to a call option written on the value of the firm, it then follows that

$$D = B(1 + r)_{-p.}^{-T} \qquad (2)$$

The value of risky debt is equal to the price of a risk-free bond with the same terms minus the price of a put written on the value of the firm.

Expression (2) has an intuitive interpretation. It is commonly understood that risky debt plus a loan guarantee has the same value as risk-free debt. The loan guarantee is like insurance, that is, it will pay any shortfall in the value of the firm necessary to fully repay the debt. Figure 5.7 depicts the value of a loan guarantee, G, on the maturity date of the risky debt. If on the maturity date of the debt the value of the firm is greater than the debt's promised principal, that is, $V > B$, then the guarantee will pay nothing since the firm is sufficiently valuable to retire the debt. However, if the value of the firm is less than the promised principal, $V < B$, then the guarantor must pay the difference between the promised principal and the value of the firm, $B - V$, in order that the debt be fully repaid. Now compare figures 5.2 and 5.7. It is evident that a loan guarantee is analogous to a European put option written on the value of the firm, that is, $G = p$. And, therefore, expression (2) is simply the statement that risky debt plus a loan guarantee is equal to a risk-free bond.

The characterization of corporate liabilities as options goes much deeper than the simple corporate securities studied so far. For example, assume

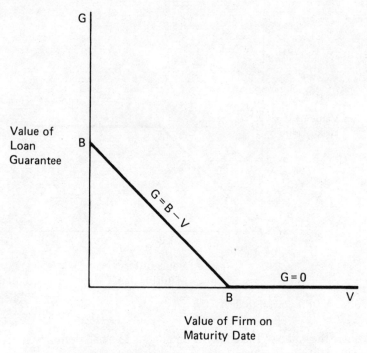

Fig. 5.7   Payoff from guaranty

that the debt receives coupon payments. Then equity can be thought of as analogous to a European call option on a dividend-paying stock where the coupon payments are the "dividends." Now assume the coupon bond is callable under a schedule of prices. The equity is now analogous to an American call option on a dividend-paying stock where the exercise price changes according to the specified schedule. Furthermore, the value of the call provision can be characterized as the difference between the value of an American and a European call option where the exercise price changes according to the specified schedule. The value of call protection against redemption for the first $T_1 < T$ time periods can be viewed as the difference between the values of two American call options on a dividend-paying stock where the first call can be exercised at any time according to a schedule and the second call can only be exercised in the last $T - T_1$ time periods. As is evident from these examples, the correspondence between corporate liabilities and options extends to a wide variety of securities and covenants.

As shown, equity, zero-coupon debt, and loan guarantees can be represented as combinations of simple option contracts. The correspondence is, moreover, sufficiently complete that it is possible to characterize many of the complex securities and covenants encountered in practice by similar analogies to basic options. Note that this correspondence is not dependent upon any particular option pricing model, but instead is a fundamental relationship which must hold independently of how options and corporate securities are assumed to be priced. Therefore, given any option pricing model with all its direct implications for pricing stock options, that same model has corresponding direct implications for the pricing of corporate liabilities and covenants.

The traditional approach to the pricing of different corporate liabilities and covenants employs different valuation techniques and rules of thumb for different problems, and rarely attempts to integrate the various components of the firm's capital structure as even a check on the internal consistency of these diverse valuation methodologies. In contrast, the CCA approach to the pricing of corporate liabilities and covenants begins with the firm's total capital structure and uses a single evaluation technique to price each of the individual components of that structure simultaneously. Thus, the CCA methodology takes into account the interactive effects of each of the securities on the prices of all the others and ensures a consistent evaluation procedure for the entire capital structure.

5.3   Call Provisions and Call Protection

JMR (1984, 1985) test the ability of a CCA model based on the option pricing principles of Black and Scholes (1973) to predict the prices of multiple issues of callable coupon debt subject to sinking funds. The test not only accounted for all the debt covenants present but also recognized the interactions among the different issues in multiple bond capital structures. Data were collected for 27 firms on a monthly basis from January 1975 through January 1981 when possible. The firms were selected according to a number of criteria at the beginning of 1975: (1) simple capital structure (i.e., one class of stock, no convertible bonds, small number of debt issues, no preferred stock); (2) small proportion of private debt to total capital; (3) small proportion of short-term notes payable or capitalized leases to total capital; and (4) all publicly traded debt is rated. Based on these criteria the following firms were selected:

Firm	Bond Rating Range	Firm	Bond Rating Range
Allied Chemical	AA/A	Cities Service	A
Anheuser Busch	A	CPC	AA/A
Braniff	BBB/CC	Crane	BBB
Brown Group	A	Food Fair	BB/B
Bucyrus Erie	A	Fuqua	B
Champion Spark Plug	AA	General Cigar	BB/B
		Kane Miller	B

Firm	Bond Rating Range	Firm	Bond Rating Range
MGM	BBB/B	Republic Steel	A
National Tea	B	Seagram	A
NVF	B	Sunbeam	A
Proctor & Gamble	AAA	Tandy	BBB/BB
Pullman	BBB	United Brands	B
Rapid American	B/CCC	Upjohn	AA
Raytheon	AA/A	Whittaker	BB/B

CCA requires three kinds of data to solve for prices of individual claims as functions of total firm value: (1) indenture data, (2) business risk data, and (3) interest rate data. For example, the following data were collected for each bond for each firm: principal, coupon rate, call price schedule, call protection period, sinking fund payments, seniority, and options to sink at market or par. The bond covenant data were collected from Moody's Bond Guide, except that sinking fund payments were collected from the monthly S&P Bond Guide. For purposes of testing the model, actual bond prices were also collected from the latter source. Business risk was estimated by measuring the volatility of the firm's equity returns and adjusting these estimates in a manner consistent with the CCA model and the observed leverage of the firm. Lastly, it was assumed that the future course of the 1-year rate of interest is known and is consistent with the 1-year forward interest rates implied by the current term structure.

Tables 5.1–5.3 summarize the results. Percentage error is defined as the predicted price minus the actual price divided by the actual price. Absolute percentage errors and results from a naive model are also reported. The naive model essentially assumes that the value of the firm is suffi-

Table 5.1   **Pricing Results and Comparisons: CCA Model and Naive (Riskless) Model (Standard Deviations in Parentheses)**

Overall Results	Number of Bonds	Mean Percentage Error		Mean Absolute Percentage Error	
		CCA Model	Naive Model	CCA Model	Naive Model
Entire sample	305	.0452	.0876	.0845	.1143
		(.1003)	(.1441)	(.1705)	(.1240)
Investment grade	176	.0047	.0149	.0587	.0574
		(.0727)	(.0703)	(.0432)	(.0432)
Noninvestment grade	129	.1005	.1867	.1197	.1919
		(.1063)	(.1590)	(.0840)	(.1528)

Table 5.2   **Individual Firm Results: CCA Model and Naive (Riskless) Model (Standard Deviations in Parentheses)**

Firm	Number of Bonds	Mean Percentage Deviation		Mean Absolute Percentage Error	
		CCA Model	Naive Model	CCA Model	Naive Model
Allied Chemical	20	−.0180	−.0155	.0616	.0598
		(.0693)	(.0678)	(.0365)	(.0357)
Anheuser Busch	20	−.0138	−.0068	.0615	.0641
		(.0760)	(.0785)	(.0467)	(.0458)
Braniff	20	.0544	.1044	.0857	.1134
		(.0957)	(.1021)	(.0691)	(.0921)
Brown Group	11	.0331	.0336	.0507	.0511
		(.0510)	(.0511)	(.0335)	(.0336)
Bucyrus Erie	10	.0187	.0228	.0313	.0331
		(.0384)	(.0372)	(.0290)	(.0283)
Champion Spark Plug	5	−.0648	−.0630	.0762	.0755
		(.0578)	(.0584)	(.0416)	(.0412)
Cities Service	10	.0262	.0308	.0553	.0557
		(.0575)	(.0541)	(.0305)	(.0278)
CPC	10	.0015	.0017	.0463	.0469
		(.0561)	(.0565)	(.0316)	(.0316)
Crane	17	.0388	.0435	.0676	.0710
		(.0758)	(.0800)	(.0518)	(.0570)
Food Fair	4	.0840	.0983	.0840	.0983
		(.0759)	(.0891)	(.0759)	(.0891)
Fuqua	22	.1048	.1658	.1195	.1802
		(.0816)	(.0908)	(.0581)	(.0571)
General Cigar	5	.0162	.0258	.0786	.0731
		(.0970)	(.0937)	(.0592)	(.0641)
Kane Miller	5	.1099	.1411	.1099	.1411
		(.0366)	(.0419)	(.0366)	(.0419)
MGM	26	.0302	.0838	.0832	.0910
		(.0922)	(.0629)	(.0501)	(.0521)
National Tea	3	.0995	.1267	.0995	.1267
		(.0511)	(.0885)	(.0511)	(.0885)
NVF	6	.1436	.2481	.1436	.2481
		(.0886)	(.0915)	(.0886)	(.0915)
Procter & Gamble	15	−.0041	−.0037	−.0492	−.0500
		(.0584)	(.0605)	(.0318)	(.0343)
Pullman	4	−.0579	−.0544	.0617	.0605
		(.0414)	(.0412)	(.0355)	(.0315)
Rapid American	22	.1565	.3832	.1579	.3832
		(.1067)	(.2084)	(.1046)	(.2084)

Table 5.2   (*continued*)

Firm	Number of Bonds	Mean Percentage Deviation		Mean Absolute Percentage Error	
		CCA Model	Naive Model	CCA Model	Naive Model
Raytheon	5	.0245	.0231	.0824	.0805
		(.0962)	(.0959)	(.0555)	(.0571)
Republic Steel	10	−.0231	.0238	.0565	.0273
		(.0647)	(.0348)	(.0391)	(.0322)
Seagram	9	.0419	.0410	.0419	.0410
		(.0283)	(.0294)	(.0283)	(.0294)
Sunbeam	5	−.0653	−.0443	.0706	.0558
		(.0513)	(.0413)	(.0436)	(.0236)
Tandy	11	.0510	.0778	.0956	.0799
		(.0951)	(.0679)	(.0501)	(.0655)
United Brands	12	.1302	.2454	.1433	.2454
		(.1423)	(.1546)	(.1291)	(.1546)
Upjohn	3	.0139	.0138	.0268	.0271
		(.0258)	(.0261)	(.0119)	(.0117)
Whittaker	15	.1129	.1529	.1286	.1529
		(.0985)	(.0713)	(.0769)	(.0713)

ciently large to make all debt riskless. These results were obtained from the same runs of the model that produced the CCA estimates. Thus the naive model prices simply reflect the magnitude and timing of promised payments discounted back by the risk-free interest rates, plus the effects of the call provision and the sinking fund option to sink at the minimum of par or market. Incrementally, the CCA model prices attempt to capture the risk of default through the consideration of business risk and financial risk, that is, finite firm value relative to promised payouts. In addition, the CCA model introduces the distinction between senior and junior debt as well as the presence of equity which complicates (relative to the naive model) the optimal call policy.

Table 5.1 presents the pricing errors for the CCA and the naive model. Results are reported for investment-grade (bond rating of BBB or higher) and non-investment-grade subsamples as well as the entire sample. As is evident from inspection, the CCA and naive models are virtually indistinguishable for investment grade bonds. This can be interpreted as evidence that default risk is not playing a significant role in explaining investment-grade bond prices. This also suggests that a stochastic interest rate model could be a better predictor of investment-grade bond prices and therefore a better predictor of the value of call provisions and call protection. There

Table 5.3   **Pricing Results and Comparisons by Year: CCA Model and Naive (Riskless) Model (Standard Deviations in Parentheses)**

Year	Number of Bonds	Mean Percentage Error		Mean Absolute Percentage Error	
		CCA Model	Naive Model	CCA Model	Naive Model
1977:					
Entire sample	60	.0906	.1470	.0918	.1475
		(.0729)	(.1833)	(.0714)	(.1830)
Investment grade	36	.0664	.0719	.0672	.0726
		(.0522)	(.0524)	(.0513)	(.0514)
Non-investment grade	24	.1269	.2598	.1287	.2598
		(.0836)	(.2423)	(.0809)	(.2423)
1978:					
Entire Sample	59	.0502	.0789	.0733	.1008
		(.0825)	(.1302)	(.0628)	(.1141)
Investment grade	35	.0102	.0132	.0486	.0502
		(.0597)	(.0605)	(.0361)	(.0363)
Non-investment grade	24	.1085	.1747	.1094	.1747
		(.0761)	(.1445)	(.0748)	(.1445)
1979					
Entire sample	62	−.0075	.0530	.0705	.0970
		(.0934)	(.1248)	(.0617)	(.0947)
Investment grade	33	−.0357	−.0223	.0568	.0497
		(.0623)	(.0628)	(.0439)	(.0443)
Non-investment grade	29	.0245	.1387	.0861	.1508
		(.1109)	(.1225)	(.0741)	(.1073)
1980					
Entire sample	63	.0607	.0994	.0943	.1253
		(.1055)	(.1370)	(.0770)	(.1138)
Investment grade	35	.0065	.0159	.0559	.0534
		(.0671)	(.0643)	(.0376)	(.0391)
Non-investment grade	28	.1285	.2039	.1422	.2152
		(.1056)	(.1320)	(.0863)	(.1126)
1981:					
Entire sample	61	.0332	.0603	.0921	.1008
		(.1135)	(.1160)	(.0741)	(.0833)
Investor grade	37	−.0263	−.0067	.0641	.0599
		(.0723)	(.0713)	(.0426)	(.0392)
Non-investment grade	24	.1249	.1637	.1353	.1637
		(.1039)	(.0935)	(.0899)	(.0935)

Table 5.4   Value of Call Provision and Call Protection: Falling Term Structure

Interest Rate Volatility	Bond Description	Par Bond Coupon
Low	Noncallable	8.625
Low	Callable after 7 years @ 100	9.06
Low	Callable after 6 years @ 100	9.06
High	Noncallable	7.875
High	Callable after 7 years @ 100	8.75
High	Callable after 6 years @ 100	9.10

do appear to be significant differences between the CCA and naive models for non-investment-grade bonds where default risk is undoubtedly playing a large role.[2]

Tables 5.2 and 5.3, which present the results by firm and year, respectively, suggest that the valuation errors could be firm and year specific. A firm effect could be induced by a specific bond effect, that is, the fact that a specific bond is underpriced in one year increases the probability it will be underpriced in other years. A firm effect could also be induced by a systematic bias in the estimate of the business risk of the firm, that is, a systematic overestimate of business risk will lead to systematic underpricing of bonds for that firm. A year effect could be induced by the nonstochastic interest rate assumption. Table 5.3 suggests that the year effect is stronger for investment grade bonds, which is consistent with viewing interest rates as the major source of uncertainty for this set of bonds. Lastly, this test of the CCA model assumed symmetric tax treatment for corporate bonds which undoubtedly explains the model's tendency to undervalue discount bonds.

One of the reasons the CCA model tested by JMR (1984) does not do a better job of predicting callable debt prices is that the model uses the value of the firm as the source of volatility, that is, default risk. As practitioners well understand, it has been the increased volatility of interest rates, not firm value, which has contributed most substantially to the overall volatility of the market. It is possible to recast the CCA model, following Cox et al. (1984), such that the source of uncertainty driving the value of such common debt covenants as call provision and call protection is interest rate risk, not default risk. Tables 5.4 and 5.5 present some CCA numeric re-

2. See Jones et al. (1984, 1985) for a more complete treatment of the differences between the CCA and naive models.

Table 5.5   **Value of Call Provision and Call Protection: Rising Term Structure**

Interest Rate Volatility	Bond Description	Par Bond Coupon
Low	Noncallable	11.50
Low	Callable after 7 years @ 100	11.50
Low	Callable after 6 years @ 100	11.50
High	Noncallable	10.31
High	Callable after 7 years @ 100	10.93
High	Callable after 6 years @ 100	11.25

sults for the value of a call provision and call protection on a risk-free bond in both a rising and a falling term structure environment. In each case it is assumed that the short-term interest rate is 10% and the bond's maturity is 10 years. In table 5.4 the term structure is assumed to be falling, with long rates at the 6% level. When interest rates have low volatility, the CCA model computes the coupon on the 10-year par bond at 8.625%. The value of the particular call provision considered, callable after 7 years at 100, is computed at 43.5 basis points (906 – 862.5). One less year of call protection is shown to have no value. When interest rates have high volatility, the CCA model computes the coupon on the 10-year bond as 7.875% and the value of the call provision as 87.5 basis points. One less year of call protection is calculated as having the value of 35 additional basis points.

Table 5.5 shows the same calculations when the term structure is rising, that is, long rates at the 15% level and the short rate at 10%. Here, logically enough, the value of the call provision and call protection is less given the upward-sloping term structure. In fact, for low volatility, the CCA model shows these provisions to have no value. In the high-volatility case, while there is some reduction in value due to the rising term structure, it is not significant. The value of the call provisions is 62 basis points and the value of one more year of call protection is 32 basis points. This underscores the relative importance of volatility versus the shape of the term structure, that is, expectations, in valuing call provisions and call protection.

5.4 Conclusion

Increased capital market volatility has increased the value of any financial flexibility built into the design of securities. The options-based CCA approach to valuing financial flexibility holds forth the potential of not only valuing a wide range of covenants but also accounting for the interaction of various securities and covenants within a capital structure. As is evident from the empirical work of JMR (1984, 1985) the application of CCA to complex capital structures is still in the development stages. However, CCA techniques are being used to help value individual covenants as demonstrated with the reported numeric analysis of call provisions and call protection. In addition, CCA is being used to value such new forms of financial flexibility as debt with warrants to purchase additional debt, puttable debt, and extendable debt. Various forms of equity-linked debt, for example, convertible debt, units of debt with warrants, exchangeable debt, and exchangeable units of debt with warrants, are also being valued using CCA techniques. While CCA is more complex than traditional valuation techniques, it more correctly incorporates the interactions of multiple securities and covenants and the role of volatility in the valuation of financial flexibility. As markets become more volatile and securities more complex, interest in correctly valuing financial flexibility should also increase.

References

Black, F., and Scholes, M. 1973. The pricing of options and corporate liabilities. *Journal of Political Economy* 81: 637–59.

Cox, J. C.; Ingersoll, J. E.; and Ross, S. A. 1985. The theory of the term structure of interest rates. *Econometrica,* 53: 385–407.

Jones, E. P.; Mason, S. P.; and Rosenfeld, E. 1984. Contingent claims analysis of corporate capital structures: an empirical investigation. *Journal of Finance* 39: 611–27.

———, 1985. Contingent claims valuation of corporate liabilities: theory and empirical test. *In The Changing Roles of Debt and Equity in Financing United States Capital Formation,* edited by B. M. Friedman. University of Chicago Press (for NBER).

Mason, S. P., and Merton, R. 1985. The role of contingent claims analysis in corporate finance. *In Recent Advances in Corporate Finance,* edited by E. I. Altmand and M. G. Subrahmanyam. New York: Irwin.

6   The Economic Effects of the Corporate Income Tax: Changing Revenues and Changing Views

Alan J. Auerbach

6.1   Introduction

Corporate income tax revenues have declined steadily as a fraction of U.S. GNP over the past three decades, from 5.3% in 1953 to 4.1%, 3.3%, and 1.8% in 1963, 1973, and 1983, respectively (Economic Report of the President 1984, tables B1, B76). Indeed, this decline is even more striking if one subtracts from corporate revenues the remittances by the Federal Reserve System of their seignorage. In fiscal 1983, corporation income tax receipts net of these payments were only $37.0 billion (Economic Report of the President 1984, table B72), or just over 6% of federal revenues.

This trend might appear to have clear implications both for the distribution of after-tax income in the United States and for the incentives that corporations have to invest in plant and equipment. But such aggregate tax measures can be very misleading because they are, at the same time, too comprehensive and yet incomplete. They do not relay the different incentives and burdens imposed on different investors and different assets, nor do they account for other taxes which, in combination with the corporate tax, determine the tax burden on owners of corporate capital and the incentives that such individuals have to invest via the corporation.

In this paper, I discuss four related issues that must be considered before the economic effects of the corporate tax can be understood. These are the additional taxes on corporate source income levied on dividends, capital gains, and interest payments; the presence in the tax code of investment incentives such as accelerated depreciation; the corporate tax treat-

Alan J. Auerbach is professor of economics at the University of Pennsylvania and a research associate of the National Bureau of Economic Research.

ment of risky income; and the determinants and implications of corporate borrowing. I conclude with a review of this discussion.

6.2 Shareholders' Taxes and "Double" Taxation

Many who favor a reduction in taxes paid by corporations see such a reduction as an offset to the "double" taxation occurring when corporate profits are taxed at the corporate level and then, if distributed, at the shareholder level. Compared to investment income from an unincorporated business, there is, indeed, a second layer of taxation. Even for earnings that are retained, associated increases in the corporation's value may eventually be subject to individual capital gains taxes.

Traditional economic analysis (e.g., Harberger 1962) suggests that such a pattern of taxation discourages corporate investment and, by doing so, causes part of the extra tax burden to be shifted from corporate shareholders to others in the economy: other investors, who find their returns diminished by the flood of capital from the corporate sector; purchasers of corporate commodities, who must pay higher prices for goods that have become more expensive to produce; and, potentially, wage earners, if the demand for labor is less intensive in the expending areas outside the corporate sector than within it.

Associated also with this hypothesized shift in resources is an economic distortion, in that investors are being encouraged by the tax system to forgo relatively more profitable corporate sector projects to avoid the extra taxation.

But the taxation of dividends does not necessarily lead to this type of outcome. The question is best put in the following way: does the taxation of dividends mean that corporations must earn a higher rate of return, before tax, to satisfy their shareholders' required after-tax return? The answer may very well be that they need not do so. Consider an investment financed by the method most commonly used to raise equity capital, the retention of earnings. Suppose the potential project will earn 10% a year after corporate taxes, all of which will be distributed as dividends. These dividends will then be subject to additional taxes, unless the shareholders are exempt from taxation. But this does not mean a lower rate of return than 10% for individual investors. Consider the initial investment these investors made when the firm retained its earnings. The cost to investors was the forgone dividends, less the taxes that would have been due on such dividends. For the sake of concreteness, suppose the typical investor's marginal tax rate is 40%. Then, per dollar of retained earnings, the investor had to give up 60 cents out of pocket to get this stream of 10% returns, which will also be taxed at 40% to yield a net return of 6% per *gross* invested dollar but 10% of forgone, after-tax dollars.

Lest this result be dismissed as anomalous, the reader should note its equivalence to the treatment accorded individual savings under a consumption tax, which is recognized to leave the return to savings effectively untaxed. Under a consumption tax scheme, savers would receive a reduction in their tax base for amounts saved through the corporation and add to the tax base amounts received and not saved.

This argument suggests that while taxes on dividends may be paid, they need not constitute a disincentive to save via the corporation. In this sense, there is no double taxation: only the corporate income tax lowers the saver's rate of return. As with a consumption tax, taxes on dividends currently received represent the payment, with interest, of a tax liability deferred by the previous retention of earnings.

A corollary of this view is that corporations face a higher marginal tax burden when they must raise equity capital through the issuance of new shares, because there is no initial reduction in stockholders' taxes when the shares are issued.

Empirical evidence offers some support for this position. In an earlier paper (Auerbach 1984), I attempted to measure how the rates of return required by corporations on their investments differed according to a number of factors, including how these investments were financed. Using data from the period 1963–77 for 274 major American corporations (most listed on the New York Stock Exchange, the remainder on the American Exchange), I first corrected income statement information to give a truer measure of annual earnings, and then estimated equations to determine the effects of a number of firm characteristics on future earnings. One significant finding was that, for given levels of investment, firms issuing new shares in a particular year experienced higher increases in earnings in subsequent years than those that invested solely through retentions and debt issues. The results suggested that this sample of firms required, on average, about 4.8% more, after tax, when financing investments through new issues. Additional evidence suggested that this phenomenon is associated with individual taxation, rather than other potential reasons for an aversion to new issues.

This finding has several interesting implications. First, corporate stock normally will trade at a discount relative to the intrinsic value of the firm's assets. This is due, not to any irrationality on the part of investors, but to the fact that firms have the incentive to retain earnings as long as the market value of new projects undertaken is at least equal to their net cost to investors. Hence, a retentions-financed project costing $1 million has a net cost of $600,000 to investors in the 40% tax bracket. The management of the firm will increase its shareholders' assets by undertaking the project as long as the firm's value increases by at least $600,000 *not* $1 million.

Second, this discount means that there is an incentive for corporations to invest in corporate stock, either their own, through repurchases, or that of others, through acquisitions. This provides a direct way of obtaining assets at a price below their intrinsic worth. The puzzle is why firms do not engage in more of this kind of activity.

Third, a general reduction in the taxation of dividend income would have very different consequences than reduced corporate taxation. Since the dividend tax does not influence the marginal tax rate for investment financed through retention, its reduction will not affect these investment decisions, despite the decline in corporate revenue.

6.3 The Impact of Investment Incentives

One reason for the decline in corporate tax collections since 1953 has been a decline in corporaate profitability. Another has been the reduction (from 52% to 46%) in the corporate tax rate. However, the most important factor has been the introduction of several investment incentives, culminating in the Accelerated Cost Recovery System instituted in 1981. For a number of reasons, the effects of these programs on the incentive to invest cannot be judged from trends in corporate tax revenues.

First, these programs were generally not retroactive. As a result, there could be relatively small change in actual tax payments in the years immediately following a new investment incentive, particularly for corporations with slower growth. However, even several years after such a program's enactment, concurrent tax payments offer little guidance about the corporation's incentive to invest. This is because investment incentives such as the investment tax credit or the shortening of depreciation lives work by reducing income taxes in the years immediately following an investment. In later years, the corporation will actually pay more taxes on the income from the investment, since depreciation allowances will have been exhausted. The net effect to the corporation is positive but is overstated by the tax reduction in the earliest years. Hence, a fast-growing corporation with a very "young" capital stock might offset all its *current* tax liability, but this will not be true in the future. A stagnant corporation with a very "old" capital stock might have no tax credits or depreciation deductions at all, but this overstates the tax burden on investment by failing to account for the tax benefits that were received in the years soon after the firm's capital goods were purchased.

In a sense, each investment faces a different tax rate on its income in each year, with this rate increasing as the asset ages. What matters for the investment decision is the present value of taxes paid over the asset's entire life, not the taxes paid in a given year.

This point may be illustrated by a numerical example. Imagine an asset purchased for $1000, yielding 20% per year before depreciation and receiving a 10% investment tax credit and a standard 5-year ACRS write-off. Suppose that the asset actually depreciates at 10% per year. That is, each year its income is 10% lower than in the previous year. Also suppose, for the sake of simplicity, that there is no inflation. Then the asset's income and tax payments over time are as given in table 6.1. Shown in parentheses below actual depreciation allowances are those that would correspond to the real or "economic" depreciation of the asset, of 10% per year. This figure is deducted from gross income to obtain a measure of actual economic income, against which taxes are compared to obtain each year's tax rate for the asset.

Because of the investment incentives, this tax rate is negative for the first 5 years but very positive thereafter. It would be no more correct to say that firms with 3-year-old assets have a tax rate of -21% (never mind how they manage to obtain these refunds—I return to this below) than that firms with 6-year-old assets face one of $+92\%$. The overall impact is somewhere in between.

This impact can be measured by taking the present value of taxes paid and finding the constant tax rate on economic income that would yield the same value. Table 6.2 (taken from Auerbach 1983) gives these calculations for two types of assets, general industrial equipment and industrial structures, and for all corporate fixed assets as a whole, for the years 1953–82. They are based under the assumptions that corporations used the most generous available tax treatment in each year, that they required a return of 4% after tax, and that they projected inflation based on past inflation behavior. Aside from the general decline in tax rates, except for a few years during the 1970s, there has been a shift in the tax burden from equipment to structures. This would appear to present the incentive for corporations to invest more in equipment, relative to structures, than is socially de-

Table 6.1	Tax Rates for a Hypothetical Asset						
	Year						
	1	2	3	4	5	6	7
Gross income	200	180	162	146	131	118	106
Depreciation allowance	143 (100)	209 (90)	200 (81)	200 (73)	200 (66)	0 (59)	0 (53)
Investment credit	100	0	0	0	0	0	0
Taxes	−74	−13	−17	−25	−32	+54	+49
Economic income	100	90	81	73	65	59	53
Tax rate (%)	−74	−14	−21	−34	−49	+92	+92

Table 6.2   Effective Tax Rates for Equipment and Structures, 1953–82 (%)

Year	General Industrial Equipment	Industrial Structures	All assets
1953	64.1	55.6	58.8
1954	61.0	52.3	55.5
1955	58.2	50.6	53.5
1956	59.3	51.3	54.3
1957	60.2	51.9	55.0
1958	60.9	52.3	55.6
1959	59.7	51.5	54.6
1960	60.4	52.0	55.1
1961	58.8	51.0	53.9
1962	40.3	49.1	43.3
1963	41.5	49.6	44.0
1964	27.4	47.1	37.2
1965	26.1	45.5	35.7
1966	27.4	45.8	36.5
1967	49.4	46.6	45.5
1968	37.0	51.5	43.5
1969	41.0	52.7	45.8
1970	53.5	52.0	49.7
1971	53.2	51.2	49.1
1972	16.4	51.2	32.9
1973	14.4	50.9	31.8
1974	18.3	51.5	33.9
1975	24.1	52.6	37.0
1976	26.4	53.1	35.1
1977	21.2	52.1	32.0
1978	23.2	52.4	33.2
1979	19.0	50.3	30.1
1980	22.0	50.8	31.9
1981	−6.8	41.7	17.7
1982	8.4	42.1	24.6

sirable, but there is an important qualification to this conclusion that will be discussed below in the section dealing with corporate borrowing.

The negative tax rate for equipment in 1981 means that the negative tax liabilities of the early years (as illustrated in table 6.1) outweighed the positive ones of later years. Such investments led to a net tax refund for investing corporations.

Aside from the distinction between these effective tax rates and those tax rates calculated by comparing current taxes to current income, there are other important implications of the presence of incentives in the tax structure. First is the increased possibility of negative tax liabilities, even for profitable firms. Because of the corporate tax treatment of losses, this may have a very unpredictable impact on the incentives for firms to invest. Second, because new assets have yet to receive their investment incentives, they will be worth more to corporations than otherwise identical but older assets already in place. Refer again to table 6.1, and imagine a company with two pieces of equipment of comparable productive capacity. One was just purchased, while the other is 6 years old. The first is clearly more valuable, because it has the prospect of 5 years of refunds before it must start paying taxes. All the older asset has in its future is years with no depreciation deductions at all. Not only does it receive no investment incentives, but it must repay the deferred taxes associated with the forward shifting of depreciation allowances.

What this means is that, per dollar of capital, existing assets will generally be worth less than new assets. The estimated extent of this discount is shown in table 6.3 (taken from Auerbach 1983). The number shown is the

Table 6.3   Ratio of Market Value to Replacement Cost: The Impact of Deferred Taxes

Year	Ratio
1953	.921
1954	.898
1955	.908
1956	.924
1957	.935
1958	.940
1959	.940
1960	.946
1961	.945
1962	.894
1963	.900
1964	.893
1965	.898
1966	.899
1967	.927
1968	.889
1969	.890
1970	.928
1971	.926
1972	.867
1973	.864
1974	.865
1975	.867
1976	.845
1977	.834
1978	.835
1979	.838
1980	.838
1981	.781
1982	.792

ratio of the total value of the aggregate corporate fixed capital stock, taking accounts of these tax differentials, to the value these assets would have if all were equally productive but treated as new assets by the tax law. Based on the size of the corporate capital stock, I calculated this gap between actual value and replacement cost to be $427 billion in 1982. This was the present value then of taxes due on old assets in excess of the taxes on comparable new assets. Combined with the capitalization effect associated with dividends, discussed in the previous section, this has the potential to explain a large gap between the intrinsic value of assets owned by corporations and their stock market values.

6.4   The Corporate Tax and Risk Taking

There are several ways in which the corporate tax affects the decision to invest in risky assets. In each case, a corporation's tax payments as a percentage of income offer little guidance about the incentives actually faced.

Perhaps the most important of these effects is associated with the corporate income tax's asymmetric treatment of a corporation's gains and losses. Income is fully taxable, but losses do not lead to a refund at the corporate rate. Instead, taxpayers must either carry the losses back for an immediate refund or, if recent income is insufficient, carry the losses forward to await deduction against future income or expiration. Further, similar restrictions exist on the use of tax credits, such as the investment tax credit.

This asymmetry means that a corporation with risky income will, in present value, pay more taxes in the future than if the income had the same expected return but were always positive. Hence, risk taking is affected. But to know *how* it is affected, one must know the firm's current tax status as well as the types of projects it is considering. Indeed, it is possible that firms with taxable income, paying taxes, are at an advantage relative to firms that are not. This is more likely given the recently increased acceleration of depreciation allowances discussed in the previous section.

While the prospect of not being able to get a refund for potential losses may discourage the undertaking of risky projects, firms that already have incurred such losses may carry forward a tax shield to reduce taxes on future income, thereby lowering taxes in the future. If, on average, the firm expected its current investments to yield additional tax liability, this shield would provide an added incentive to invest. However, as shown by the example in table 6.1, many investments now will generate negative tax liabilities in their early years, even if they earn a normal rate of return. Hence, a tax shield carried forward may actually make such investments less attractive by making the deduction of these additional losses impossible. This is offset by the fact that in subsequent years, when the assets generate positive tax liabilities, these are more likely to be shielded from taxation.

To measure the net impact of these effects, I considered (Auerbach 1983) how the expected present value of taxes associated with different assets would be affected by a firm's initial tax status and the probability that this tax status would change from year to year. Using data from 1959 to 1978 for several hundred major U.S. corporations, I estimated the probability of having a net tax loss carry-forward in any given year and the probability that this loss would be exhausted in the next and subsequent years. I then measured the taxes that representative firms, purchasing an asset with a riskless, 6% return annually after depreciation, would expect to pay in each year over the asset's life. Each calculation proceeded in two steps. First, the annual accrued tax liability for each year, such as those shown in table 6.1, was calculated. Then, estimates were made of when, statistically, each of these liabilities would actually result in a tax payment. Since a firm might have a tax loss carry-forward (from other parts of its operations) in each year, there is some probability that each year's tax payment would be deferred, more so for firms beginning with a large tax loss carry-forward in the year of the investment.

To test the effect of different conditions on the results, I performed these calculations for both industrial equipment and industrial structures; for zero, medium, and high rates of inflation; and under depreciation provisions that existed in 1965, 1972, and 1982. For each assumption of asset types, inflation rate, and tax law, the calculation was done for two representative corporations: one starting off with a substantial current tax liability and the potential for a tax loss carry-back, and one beginning with a large tax loss carry-forward. These firms are labeled "high tax" and "low tax" for the results shown in table 6.4. The numbers in the table are

Table 6.4   Effective Tax Rates: The Importance of Deferred Payment, by Taxable Status (%)

Tax Law and Inflation Rate	General Industrial Equipment		Industrial Structures	
	Low Tax	High Tax	Low Tax	High Tax
1965 tax law:				
No inflation	17	12	37	37
4%	33	30	48	48
8%	47	43	53	53
1972 tax law:				
No inflation	12	7	40	38
4%	28	23	52	52
8%	40	35	57	57
1982 tax law:				
No inflation	-3	-15	27	25
4%	10	-3	37	35
8%	20	5	42	42

"effective" tax rates, as described above, calculated as the tax rate on economic income that would leave firms with the same expected present value of taxes from the investment.

The table offers a number of familiar results. For each type of investor and asset, the tax changes from 1972 to 1982 led to lower tax liabilities. For any given asset, investor, and year, an increase in the inflation rate led to higher tax payments because of the declining real value of depreciation allowances. As depicted above, recent tax changes have greatly increased the relative tax incentive to invest in equipment instead of structures.

The main new result in the table is that firms in the "high tax" position were likely to pay less in taxes on their new investments than their "low tax" counterparts, because of the greater likelihood of obtaining the full value of the early years' negative tax liabilities. This has become especially true for equipment since the most recent tax law changes. Hence, the observation of one firm paying a larger fraction of its earnings in taxes than another is certainly a poor guide to the relative incentives for these firms to undertake new investment.

An implication of these findings is that those firms with existing profitable operations providing taxable income are better disposed to undertake new investments, either directly or through the purchase of other firms making these investments. Once again, the tax system provides an extra incentive for the acquisition of one firm by another.

6.5   Determinants of Corporate Leverage

An element of corporate policy that adds to each of the preceding ones and helps tie them together is the debt-equity decision. While the advantages of retaining earnings instead of issuing new shares are fairly clear, the decision of how much growth to finance internally and how much through the flotation of debt has many interesting and complex aspects. There are theories to explain how much corporations borrow, when they borrow, and the maturity structure of their borrowing, but these theories are often incomplete predictors of actual behavior.

The tax law plays a central role in most models of corporate leverage, and its recent changes motivate some of the current interest in the question of what determines corporate borrowing. As shown above in sections 6.3 and 6.4, estimates suggest that the effective tax rates on structures lie substantially above those on equipment. Further, nondepreciable assets, such as land and inventories, do not qualify for any investment incentives comparable to those available for plant and equipment. This suggests that there exists a potentially serious distortion in the choice of corporate investments, but such a conclusion is necessarily valid only if a separation prevails between real and financial corporate decisions. If, in contrast, there are tax advantages to borrowing, and leverage is more acceptable to corporations when investing in structures or land than in equipment, this might offset the tax disadvantage of the former assets to which we have already alluded.

In another paper (Auerbach 1985), I estimated models of the determinants of corporate borrowing. Before discussing the actual results, it will be useful to review briefly some of the theories that lie behind the model.

Most theories of corporate leverage begin with the twin observations that corporate taxation appears to bias the choice of financial policy completely toward debt and that corporations typically finance perhaps only one-quarter of their accumulations of capital by issuing debt. The challenge is to explain why this is so.

The most basic explanation for observed debt-equity ratios is costly bankruptcy. However, empirical evidence tends to refute the notion that potential bankruptcy costs alone are of the same magnitude as the corporate tax advantage to debt. Moreover, additional borrowing may lead to other costs, referred to in the finance literature as "agency" costs, associated with the idea that it is difficult for holders of long-term bonds in a firm to protect themselves from the firm's taking subsequent action that is detrimental to their interests, such as the commencement of an extremely risky new investment program. With limited corporate liability, this act imparts some of the program's risk to holders of debt. In anticipation of such behavior, lenders might demand a high-risk premium from firms with a high probability of engaging in such activity, such as firms with high debt-equity ratios.

One would expect a firm's potential agency costs to differ according to a number of characteristics in addition to its debt-equity ratio. Myers (1977) suggests that the problem is more acute for "growth" firms whose value derives largely from anticipated future decisions, since they possess more flexibility in their actions. Presumably the same argument holds for firms whose capital stock has a short maturity, for these firms' future replacement investment decisions loom much larger. This could be a reason for firms that use structures relatively more than equipment in their production processes to borrow more, or at least borrow more long term.

Additional explanations for the limitation on corporate borrowing come from suggestions that other *tax* factors act, cumulatively, to offset the tax advantage to borrowing, so that at a certain point the net tax advantage to borrowing disappears. At the corporate level, the tax advantage to debt is lost if firms do not have sufficient taxable income to deduct their interest payments. As firms borrow more and attempt to deduct more interest, this eventuality becomes ever more likely. This is the essence of the argument offered by DeAngelo and Masulis (1980). The hypothesis has a number of testable implications. First, firms with substantial loss carry-forwards should choose to issue less debt. (Care must be taken since such firms may also be in greater need of funds.) Second, firms investing in assets with a greater fraction of their total after-tax returns generated by tax credits and deductions should also use less debt finance, for they typically will have less taxable income for any given level of borrowing. Again, this is a reason why firms might borrow less to finance purchases of equipment. Finally, one would expect that firms with riskier earnings streams would be less likely to borrow, for these firms would face a more likely prospect of having insufficient taxable income, in any given year, to deduct all interest payments.

As with the pure bankruptcy explanation, this "limited tax shield" argument, by itself, is unlikely to be important enough to explain the typical firm's observed borrowing behavior. As part of the study of tax losses (Auerbach 1983), I estimated the present value of tax deductions from an additional dollar of debt for a typical firm and found that such a firm could expect to get about 92% of the value of these deductions. Equivalently, this would be as if firms could deduct interest payments regardless of their own tax status, but at a 42% rather 46% tax rate. This is still a substantial tax benefit.

However, this differential is diminished by the consideration of personal taxes. Miller (1977) argued that the individual tax advantages to equity may offset those to debt at the firm level. The basic argument is that since, at the individual level, interest payments are taxable, while only dividends and not capital gains are taxed fully, the individual tax burden on the return to equity is lower than that on debt. In its simplest form this explanation is implausible, since the corporate tax on all equity earnings plus the additional dividend taxation of that part of the individual return to equity that is distributed to shareholders is substantially higher than the individual tax on interest income, regardless of the individual's tax bracket. However, this effect may lessen the initial tax advantage to leverage and, in conjunction with other reasons for limits on leverage given above, may help explain observed behavior.

Moreover, as argued above in section 6.2, though individual stockholders pay taxes on dividends, these taxes do not necessarily constitute a burden on the current return to equity. Because the value of the firm may be discounted to account for the presence of the dividend tax, the tax itself does not lower the return on investment for an equity holder. This point makes Miller's original argument more realistic, for it means that the only additional taxation of equity earnings besides the corporate tax itself is the individual capital gains tax.

In summary, explanations for borrowing limitations range over tax and nontax factors. Among the latter are the potential bankruptcy and agency costs that are thought to derive from additional leverage. Among the former are the limited deductibility of additional interest payments by the corporate borrower and the offsetting tax advantages to equity at the individual level.

To test these different theories, I gathered balance sheet and income statement data for the period 1958–77 on 143 firms for which sufficient information was available about capital stock composition. All of the firms chosen listed annual investment and capital stocks separately for three categories: structures, land, and equipment.

As in the calculations described in section 6.2, the first step was to correct several book measures, such as earnings and debt. The former had to be corrected for inventory valuation and capital consumption adjustments, and the latter for deviations from market value associated with interest rate changes.

Once this was done, I used the data from all of the firms to estimate models of short-term and long-term borrowing. The models specify that there is, for each firm, a desired ratio of short-term debt to total value and long-term debt to total value. The annual borrowing decision is modeled as being one of partial adjustment, with the change in each ratio of debt to value depending on three factors: the gap between desired long-term debt and its current level, the gap between desired short-term debt and its current level, and the "cash flow" gap between current investment funds needed and the amount of funds available through retentions after a normal dividend distribution. Hence, the amount of long-term (or short-term) borrowing is hypothesized to be influenced by how much long-term debt the firm would like to add, how much short-term debt it would like to add, and how much debt overall it must add if it is not to reduce its dividend growth or issue new equity shares.

The estimated equations indicate that firms close about 44% of the gap between desired and actual long-term debt-value ratios within a year but that short-term borrowing responds more rapidly, closing over 79% of the gap between desired and actual levels within a year. Both forms of borrowing respond positively to the size of the cash flow deficit, and short-term debt appears to increase also when there is a desire for more long-term debt, indicating a degree of substitutability between the two forms of borrowing.

We turn next to the determinants of desired debt-value ratios. For both long-term and short-term debt, I estimated the impact of a number of firm characteristics. Included in this group are the tax loss carry-forward (if present), the earnings growth rate, the variance of earnings (adjusted for borrowing) around trend, and the fraction of the firm's value accounted for by land, structures, equipment, net current assets (including inventories), and goodwill, respectively. The last fraction is simply defined as the residual difference between the aggregate replacement value of the firm's assets in the other four categories and the market value of the firm itself. This is intended to measure future earnings prospects, among other things.

There are many factors estimated to affect significantly the desired debt-value ratios, but only some are consonant with the theories laid out above. As expected, land appears to be the most heavily leveraged of all assets, and goodwill is less associated with borrowing than land, equipment, or current assets. However, for both long-term and short-term debt, the assets that are estimated to have the lowest associated debt-equity ratios are structures. This is a puzzle for which I have no ready explanation. Also puzzling is the *positive* impact on leverage of a firm's growth rate, although here it must be recalled that all of the firms studied are large, blue chip corporations. In this context, "growth company" does not have the usual connotation of being a speculative enterprise. Finally, the effects of earnings variance and tax loss carry-forwards on leverage are not especially perceptible.

Thus, the results offer no support for the proposition that companies investing primarily in structures borrow more than companies investing in equipment, though land does seem to have greater associated borrowing. The separation between real and financial decisions does not appear to hold, but no combination of the theories reviewed above is sufficient to explain this borrowing pattern completely. Hence, it is difficult to know how to bring the tax advantage to debt into calculations of overall tax incentives facing investments of different types, though it appears there is a substantial tax advantage to investing in equipment rather than structures.

6.6 Conclusions

I have discussed in each of the sections above how the impact of the corporate tax is difficult to measure from observed revenue figures alone. It will be useful to summarize them here.

First, the existence of "double taxation" of dividends is highly questionable. The payment of dividend taxes does not mean that these taxes affect the returns to current investors, because the taxes will already be reflected in the firm's market value via a discount relative to the intrinsic value of the firm's assets. Second, investment incentives defer tax payments by corporations, so that income from newer assets is taxed less heavily than that from older assets. This makes aggregate corporate tax payments meaningless as economic indicators. Because of the relatively bigger tax shield offered by new investments, older assets will carry a discount in the determination of a corporation's market value, leading to a second tax-associated cause for the presence of a discount in the value of corporate equity.

The riskiness of corporate investments combined with the asymmetry of the corporate tax in its treatment of gains and losses means that the corporation's incentive to invest depends on its tax status. Given the negative accrued tax liabilities in the early years after an investment is made, associated with investment tax credits and accelerated depreciation, the incentive to invest is greater for a firm that is currently taxable than for a firm that is not.

Finally, the financial decision, if not made separately from the real investment decision, may influence the investment choice among various assets. Observed behavior indicates that financial and real decisions are related, but not strictly according to any pattern predicted by prevailing theories.

References

Auerbach, A. J. 1983. Corporate taxation in the U.S. *Brookings Papers on Economic Activity* 14 (February): 451–505.

———. 1984. Taxes, firm financial policy, and the cost of capital: an empirical analysis. *Journal of Public Economics* 23 (February/March): 27–57.

———. 1985. Real determinants of corporate leverage. In *Corporate Capital Structures in the U.S.,* edited by B. Friedman. Chicago: University of Chicago Press (for NBER).

DeAngelo, H., and Masulis, R. 1980. Optimal capital structure under corporate and personal taxation. *Journal of Financial Economics* 8 (March): 3–81.

Economic Report of the President. 1984. Washington, D.C.: Government Printing Office.

Harberger, A. C. 1962. The incidence of the corporation income tax. *Journal of Political Economy* 70 (May): 261–75.

Miller, M. H. 1977. Debt and taxes. *Journal of Finance* 32, (May): 261–75.

Myers, S. 1977. Determinants of corporate borrowing. *Journal of Financial Economics* 5 (November): 147–75.

Contributors

Alan J. Auerbach
Department of Economics
University of Pennsylvania
3718 Locust Walk/CR
Philadelphia, PA 19104

Zvi Bodie
School of Management
Boston University
704 Commonwealth Avenue
Boston, MA 02215

Benjamin M. Friedman
Department of Economics
Harvard University
Littauer Center 127
Cambridge, MA 02138

Patric H. Hendershott
Hagerty Hall
1775 College Road
Ohio State University
Columbus, OH 43210

Alex Kane
Department of Finance and Economics
Boston University
704 Commonwealth Avenue
Boston, MA 02215

Scott P. Mason
Graduate School of Business
  Administration
Harvard University
Boston, MA 02163

Robert McDonald
Graduate School of Management
Northwestern University
Leverone Hall
Evanston, IL 60201

Robert A. Taggart, Jr.
School of Management
Boston University
704 Commonwealth Avenue
Boston, MA 02215

Index